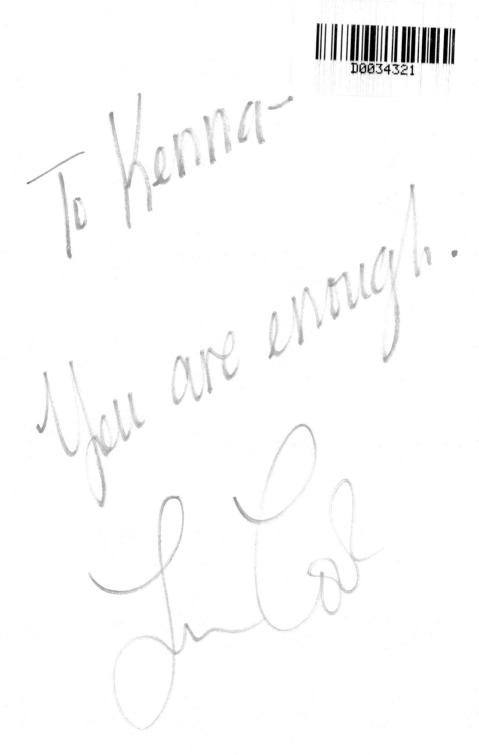

To Kenna—

You are enough.

NAME YOUR STORY

HOW TO TALK OPENLY ABOUT MENTAL HEALTH WHILE EMBRACING WELLNESS

LAUREN COOK

NAME YOUR STORY
How to Talk Openly About Mental Health While Embracing Wellness

iUniverse books may be ordered through booksellers or by contacting:

iUniverse
1663 Liberty Drive
Bloomington, IN 47403
www.iuniverse.com
1-800-Authors (1-800-288-4677)

ISBN: 978-1-5320-1809-1 (sc)
ISBN: 978-1-5320-1810-7 (e)

Library of Congress Control Number: 2017902847

Print information available on the last page.

iUniverse rev. date: 03/29/2017

For Greg:
Thank you for being my light and inspiration.

"I am not afraid of storms for I am learning how to sail my ship."
Louisa May Alcott

Contents

Introduction

Our society is inundated with the message that we need to be happy all the time. I would know—I've been studying happiness since college. For a long time I bought into the message that we should be happy no matter what. And while I am still an advocate for positivity, I now know that happiness is just one piece of the emotional pie. When we focus solely on positive emotions, we often neglect the more painful emotions that are just as present in our lives. As authentic people, we experience a whole range of emotions—frustration, disappointment, ecstasy, boredom, and doubt, just to name a few. The more in touch we can get with each of these emotions, the more equipped we are to handle whatever we may have experienced or are yet to face.

The Emotional Pie

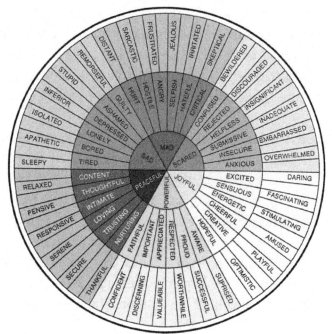

Image credit to Dr. Gloria Willcox

What emotions do you feel like you experience on a regular basis?

_____

_____

_____

What emotions do you feel like you rarely experience?

_____

_____

_____

It's no surprise that we have come to believe that happiness is the only acceptable emotion to feel or display to others. We are flooded by our social media accounts showing waves of people smiling, laughing, and living the most extraordinary lives. Or so it seems. It's rare that we see posts commenting on the stress of schoolwork, the loneliness of a Tuesday night, or fights with parents or loved ones. And while the world doesn't need to be on speed-dial for all our setbacks, it's that much more challenging when we feel like we are alone in our struggles.

The good news is that we are not alone—far from it. Each of us endures our own personal setbacks and the sooner we can come together in these hardships, the more we can heal. You may feel like you're the only one who isn't always happy, but the truth is, one in 25% of teens experience some form of anxiety and 12.5% will experience depression.[1],[2] One in four college students experience a mental health challenge.[3] This means that if you are not going through a personal hardship, chances are your friend, family member, classmate, neighbor, or roommate may be going through something and might need help.

No matter where you are in life, striving towards better mental health will always be a worthy goal. Before I proceed, I want to specifically define what mental health is. According to MentalHealth. gov, "mental health includes our emotional, psychological, and social wellbeing, which affects how we think, feel, and act. It also helps us determine how to handle stress, relate to others, and make choices."[4] That's a pretty solid definition, but we have to think about how this applies to our lives personally. Just like our fitness level, our mental health can vary throughout our lives; sometimes we feel emotionally strong, and other times, we can feel unstable. It's important to keep a pulse on how you're doing so that you stay aware of any changes in your mental health.

What does mental health mean to you?

_____

_____

_____

How mentally healthy do you feel presently?

_____

_____

Throughout your life, how has your mental health varied? How so?

_____

_____

_____

I know that talking about mental health can be overwhelming and scary, especially the first time around. We don't know what to say—we are worried we will sound awkward, uninformed, and we may even be afraid of making someone angry or hurting their feelings. Yet the more we educate ourselves, the more prepared we are to handle these real conversations. It may not always be easy but leaning into the dialogue is always worth it. It could even save someone's life.

This book is here to inform and support you through your journey towards mental health and to help those around you. We are all doing the best that we can, and the more supportive and understanding we can be with each other, the better off we will all be. My hope is that this book can provide a place for you to process your own feelings while you learn more about mental health and wellbeing. Unfortunately, there are a lot of myths and misperceptions about mental health and it is my goal to clarify and provide the facts up front. You deserve to be informed and I believe we owe it to ourselves and others to have the most reliable information possible. I look forward to walking through this journey towards mental health together, one step at a time.

My Harry Potter Moment

If you were born in the 90's or after, you grew up with Harry Potter. No exception, I loved reading every book in the series and I would go to the midnight release parties in full wardrobe with wand in hand. Even though I'm a self-declared Hufflepuff, I always admired Harry's fearlessness. One scene that has always stood out to me is the night Harry learns about what happened to his parents when he was a baby. Hagrid tries to say the name of the evil wizard but stutters before eventually saying his name—*Voldemort*. Without hesitation, Harry repeats the name back loudly. He does not express cowardice in that moment—nor did he for the rest of the story. He always named "He-Who-Must-Not-Be-Named," and he looked Voldemort in the eyes several times before conquering him. Harry never shied away from the wizard who tried to encapsulate fear and terror within him—instead he faced him, without hesitation.

We need to face mental health with this same bravery. Somehow our society has termed words like "depression," "anxiety," and especially "suicide" as words that must not be spoken. They are the Voldemorts that must be ignored, hid, and avoided. However, shying away from them just gives them that much more power. They become words that have stigma and shame attached, because we are too afraid to voice them publicly. We think that those who experience symptoms like hopelessness or agitation are "broken," "crazy," or "weird" because they may seem different or "not normal." We think that they should be left out, excluded, and isolated because they do not seem perfectly put together all the time.

We need to find our inner Harry and start becoming comfortable naming the words that we are afraid to say. The moment we can say words like "depression," "anxiety," and "suicide," they begin to lose their power to instigate fear. These words can no longer cripple us into silence. It's okay to say, "I live with anxiety and I am working to improve on a daily basis" or "I have an eating disorder and I am trying to get help." It's even okay to say, "I feel suicidal and I need help." We become empowered when we can take ownership of our experience and name what is challenging us. It is only at that point when we have "named it" that we can begin to receive help.

We also learn that those who are struggling are not "strange" or "inept." They simply have their own battles to conquer and the best thing we can do is support them so that they come out victorious. The only way to fight the stigma is if we are willing to say what we have experienced and show others that, despite the struggle, we are still standing. We are still here. And no matter what others may say, we can succeed and excel beyond their expectations. We are incredibly strong.

Here is your opportunity to **Name It***. Is there anything that you have been struggling with recently or in the past?*

_____

_____

_____

Have you been able to tell others about this challenge? If you haven't been able to talk about it, what is preventing you from sharing this information with a safe person?

_____

_____

_____

In the coming chapters I will name and describe some of the more common conditions that young adults experience so that you can become aware of any feelings within yourself or within others.

This is not a book to diagnose (as you should meet with a mental health professional for diagnosis) but rather a book to inform. This book is meant to serve as a toolkit to help guide you as you may begin having questions, thoughts, or concerns.

It is a great relief when we can name our experience—whatever it might be. We each have our own Voldemort that we are battling, but the second we can say it out loud, we often feel a tremendous amount of relief. We are no longer held prisoner to our fear and we learn that we do not have to feel so alone anymore. I know it takes courage to face whatever it is that may feel scary—especially when it is happening for the first time—but know that others have endured similar struggles and have overcome time and time again. You will, too.

Of course, maybe you are reading this and thinking, "I feel completely fine. There is nothing wrong right now." That's perfectly okay, too! Even if you are not experiencing a challenge with your mental health, it's still so important that you take the time to learn about it. Because whether you have a problem later in life or you encounter someone who is experiencing a hardship, this information about mental health will be pertinent to you someday. The best thing you can do is to take a preventative approach and learn as much as you can now. You never know when you might need it.

I've Named It. Now What?

The next step is facing it. While the first step is naming it, the next part is learning how to deal with it. In the following chapters, we will talk about the best ways to cope with mental health challenges and how to employ self-care. It is crucial that we invest time in ourselves and learn how to treat ourselves with compassion. We'll also talk about how to have healthy conversations with those that we care about. Perhaps a family member, someone you are dating, or friend is causing you concern. How do you talk about it with them? Or someone approaches you because they are worried about your wellbeing. How do you hear what they have to say without feeling defensive or attacked? We'll cover all angles of this so that you can maneuver these conversations while still remaining close with the people you care about.

It is much easier to operate in a place of denial when we are struggling. If we pretend it's not there, maybe it will go away. Chances are, it won't. In fact, denial only feeds the problem and helps it grow bigger. As counterintuitive as it may feel, we need to pay attention to our setbacks if we want to advance forward. Sometimes it can be a painful process to look at the reasons why we are hurting but if we are willing to look at our pain and understand why we are feeling it, we can begin to heal ourselves. What's more, when you've gone through the work of restoring yourself, you will be so much better equipped the next time you feel triggered or a problem comes up (because it will). Adversities will inevitably come up, but the way you respond is ultimately your choice. It is within your capacity to change.

My hope is that this book helps you develop stronger emotional muscles. The best way to do that is to face what you are feeling— especially if those feelings are causing you stress, upset, or sadness. If you are willing to engage in the process, you will not live in nearly as much discomfort or fear. Sir Frances Bacon said that knowledge is power and when it comes to mental health, it certainly is. While I cannot take away the painful feelings you may feel, I can provide you with information that will help you to learn what you do with those feelings. Once you are able to take action with your emotions—rather than feel like you are a victim to them—you will likely feel a greater sense of relief and enjoyment out of life.

I'm Facing It. Now What?

The final step in this journey is embracing your experience with mental health. Everyone's story is different and when we can acknowledge who we are and the way we feel, we are on a path to wellbeing. Reaching this point of acceptance does not happen overnight. It takes time to process what we are feeling and we need to come to terms with expectations that may potentially go unmet. We often hold ourselves to such high (and unattainable) standards that learning we are not perfect, tireless, or without hardship can be difficult to appreciate sometimes. This journey can't be rushed. My hope is that as you go along, you can continually to work toward a place of self-acceptance.

Facing our challenges does not relegate us to a life of failure. A common misconception is that those who struggle with their mental health are determined to have setback after setback. This couldn't be further from the truth. Just because someone is diagnosed with Bipolar Disorder, Obsessive Compulsive Disorder, or Anorexia Nervosa, for example, does not mean they cannot have an incredible and yes, happy, life. One of my favorite examples of this is Dr. Elyn Saks. She is the Associate Dean and Professor of Law at the University of Southern California and attended Yale Law School, among many other accolades. Oh, let me mention one more detail: she has schizophrenia. Her book, *The Center Cannot Hold*, is an incredible autobiography about her trials and tribulations but more importantly, about her will to overcome regardless of the obstacles.[5] She is a force to be reckoned with and she is not going to let something like schizophrenia stop her from reaching her potential.

I hear numerous stories like this on a daily basis. People are not only living with, but also thriving, in the midst of a variety of mental health challenges and I believe that it is because they have named it, faced it, and embraced it. Whether you are experiencing this personally or know someone who is, I'm glad that you are joining me as we work towards better mental health for all.

Embrace It: Developing Emotional Intelligence

Ultimately, I hope that after you read this book you will gain a greater sense of what mental health means to you and how you can improve it in your life. One way we can do this by expanding upon our Emotional Intelligence. I love how Goldie Hawn and Wendy Holden reference this concept in their book, *Ten Mindful Minutes*.[6] What does Emotional Intelligence include?

- **Self-awareness:** knowing what we think and feel, and how these thoughts and feelings impact our choices and actions.
- **Self-management:** learning how to deal with difficult emotions so that they don't lead to challenges; able to establish goals and handle struggles.
- **Responsible decision-making:** able to think of solutions to problems and think of the consequences from our choices, both for our own lives and for others.
- **Social awareness:** understanding the thoughts, feelings, and perspectives of others while fostering empathy.
- **Relationship skills:** being able to handle conflicts; having close connections to other people while resisting negative peer influences.

Sometimes it's hard to grasp these concepts when they're in definition format. Here's an **Emotional Intelligence Assessment** to help you apply this to your own life. This is a great quiz from Mind Tools that I like to use.[7] Remember that it's not a make or break score, it's just meant to help you get a ball park figure for how emotionally in tune you are with yourself and others.

For each statement, evaluate how you actually are, rather than what you feel you should be.	Not At All (1 point)	Rarely (2 points)	Sometimes (3 points)	Often (4 points)	Very Often (5 points)
1. I can recognize my emotions as I experience them.					
2. I stay calm even when I feel frustrated.					

For each statement, evaluate how you actually are, rather than what you feel you should be.	Not At All (1 point)	Rarely (2 points)	Sometimes (3 points)	Often (4 points)	Very Often (5 points)
3. People have told me that I'm a good listener.					
4. I know how to calm myself down when I feel anxious or upset.					
5. I enjoy organizing groups.					
6. I am able to focus on something over the long term.					
7. I know my strengths and weaknesses.					
8. I am not afraid of conflict and negotiations.					
9. I enjoy school and/or work.					
10. I ask people for feedback on what I do well, and how I can improve.					
11. I set long-term goals, and review my progress regularly.					
12. I am able to read other people's emotions.					
13. I am able to build rapport with others.					
14. I use active listening skills when people speak to me.					
15. I am able to move on even though I have been feeling frustrated or unhappy.					

All finished? Go ahead and calculate your score. For example, if you marked "Very Often" 15 times, your score would be 75 (5 points x 15 questions) or if you answered "Not At All" to 15 questions, your score would be 15 (1 point x 15 questions).

What was your score? _____

Here is the score guide:

15-34 points: It's a good idea to spend some time working on your emotional intelligence. You might be feeling overwhelmed by your emotions, especially when you're stressed out. You might also find yourself avoiding conflicts because it is extra upsetting for you. You may have a harder time calming down when you feel upset and it might be harder for you to form strong relationships. There are many things you can do to increase your emotional intelligence and we'll talk about that later on.

35-55 points: Your emotional intelligence is okay, but there is still room for improvement. You likely have good relationships with some people in your life, but you struggle to get along with others. The good news is that you can always grow and your emotional intelligence can increase.

56-76 points: You're very emotionally intelligent. You maintain great relationships with others and people probably seek you out for help and advice. Remember though that you shouldn't forget about our own emotional needs! We'll talk about how you can balance helping others while still taking care of yourself.

Were you surprised by your score? Why or why not?

_____

_____

What are your strengths when it comes to your emotional intelligence?

_____

_____

What can you improve upon regarding your emotional intelligence?

_____

_____

_____

So what now? The amazing thing about emotional intelligence is that it is never static—it is never fixed. We often have the misconception that our intelligence is at a set point and there's only so much we can improve. This couldn't be further from the truth, especially when it comes to emotional intelligence. Throughout your life, you can always keep building your awareness for yourself and others. It is so important to be mindful of your wellbeing because it directly correlates with your mental health. The more in tune you are with your physical, mental, and emotional health, the more you will be able to help both yourself and others. We'll working throughout the remainder of the book on different ways that you can grow your emotional intelligence. Here aare some snapshot ideas:

Self-awareness:

- *Practice mindfulness.* This is when you focus on the present moment and note how you are feeling. You are in touch with the "right here, right now" and you are not keeping track of time.
- *Keep a journal where you log your emotional experiences that day.* Write vividly about the way that you felt and recall the physical

sensations of the experience. This will help feel more in touch with your body and your surroundings.

- *Note the highs and lows of your day.* When you're having dinner with your family or before you go to bed each night, have each person in your family share what the "high" (best part of the day) along with the "low" (hardest part of the day). Some families also like to add a "surprise" moment of the day as well for an extra twist.

What can I do to increase my self-awareness?

_____

_____

Self-management:

- *Practice deep breathing to help yourself calm down when feeling stressed.* This is especially great if you feel a bout of anger coming on. Take at least five deep breaths in one sitting. It's even better if you can lay down and feel your belly breathing or sit against a wall to focus on the movement.
- *Take a walk.* It's best to remove yourself from a situation if you notice that you are feeling triggered. Get some fresh air and move your body. This will help break up any tension building in your muscles.
- *Move your hands.* When negative feelings are brewing in your body, find a way to channel some of that energy. Some people love using a stress ball, play dough, or silly putty as a way to do this. For other people, balling up their fists and then releasing the tension works as well.

What can I do to increase my self-management skills?

_____

_____

Responsible decision-making:

* *Create at least five long-term goals that you have in the next year.* Write them down and then place these goals in an area where you can see them. This will help you stay on target so that you don't get distracted.

* *Make a daily to-do list.* It's so easy to get caught up in the menial tasks that we have to deal with on a regular basis. Each day, spend five minutes writing down everything that you have to get done. This will help your mind organize how to shape your day. If you're feeling especially overwhelmed, highlight the top three most important tasks and focus solely on those three goals before you move on to other assignments.

* *Find a mentor.* When you have someone looking out for you and providing accountability, it's a lot harder to let them down. It's important to know that people care about your success and bringing a mentor into your life will help you reach new levels. You'd be surprised how many people are willing to help shape you, whether that applies to your schooling, career, or personal life. People want to see you succeed.

What can I do to improve my decision-making skills?

_____

_____

Social awareness:

- *Put your phone down when people are speaking to you.* The best way to engage with someone who is speaking to you is to make direct eye contact with them. You will form much stronger connections with people when a screen isn't coming between the two of you.
- *Watch body language.* There is so much that people don't say when they are speaking. If you watch their gestures and even listen to the tone of their voice, you'll become aware of what they are actually trying to communicate.
- *Ask questions.* If you want to truly understand someone (and help them feel cared about), then ask thoughtful questions. This expresses your interest and concern for a person and it will help them open up to you more. You'll also feel much more engaged in the conversation because you will become invested in the experience.

What can I do to increase my social awareness?

_____

_____

Relationship skills:

- *Invite friends to spend quality time with you.* One of the best ways to build stronger relationships is to engage in meaningful activities with friends. Make memories with people that you care about. Try new restaurants, go for a bike ride, or engage in other activities that bring you joy when you're with loved ones. Don't just "hang out" where you sit together staring at screens—that doesn't count as quality time.
- *Approach someone directly when you are having a conflict.* You may be tempted to engage in gossip or have a physical fight

with the person you're having a problem with but the best thing you can do is to talk it out with them. While you cannot control what their reaction will be, you can know that you did the mature thing by appropriately confronting the person rather than avoiding them.

- *Learn to walk away.* It's easy to feel pressured into doing things you don't want to do. This could be everything from going to a party when you just want to stay home to taking another AP class because "all your friends are doing it." But any social judgment that may come your way because you said "no" is not your problem—it's theirs. Trust me when I say that the momentary FOMO (fear of missing out) you might have will be quickly replaced by a wave of relief. It feels good to follow your gut and do what is best for you.

What can I do to improve my relationship skills?

_____

_____

Keep these ideas about emotional intelligence in your back pocket as we go through the book. I realize that it can be a lot of information to manage at once, but I think that emotional intelligence can be an excellent way to ground yourself when you are feeling overwhelmed. Sometimes the text can feel triggering or upsetting and if you feel a reaction like that coming on, step away from the book for a little while and practice some of these emotionally intelligent skills. This will center you and bring you back to a safe place. You don't need to push yourself or make yourself feel uncomfortable. Go at a pace that is natural for you and give yourself as much time as you need to process how you're feeling.

What's Going On Here?

Being a young adult is hard enough as it is. You're under an incredible amount of stress with homework, sports, dancing, having a job—you name it, every hour of your day is packed. It can be so stressful when you're trying to get by day-to-day, or even from one hour to the next.

I meet a lot of student on the road who tell me their lives feel like a washing machine cycle. They wake up, go to class, go play soccer/dance (insert your activity here), do some homework, maybe take a shower, and do it all over again. Rinse, repeat. Rinse, repeat. With a lifestyle like this, we're always wishing for the next Saturday because every day becomes such a grind. How do we break up the monotony?

If you don't establish healthy coping skills, each day can feel harder and harder. Not to mention, with each passing year, there are even more obligations. By the time you're in high school, there is so much pressure to get into college. Then, by the time you're in college, you're feeling the heat to get a stellar internship or job. It feels never-ending. And while we all experience varying amounts of stress, sometimes it can go into overdrive. We may have different reactions to upsetting circumstances than we used to as a child and this may take us by surprise. When we're going through our adolescent and young adult years, things like depression, anxiety, or other conditions may emerge for the first time, and if we're not aware of what they are, we can feel scared, alone, and worried.

What are some potential reasons that you may be having a different reaction than the "usual?" Here is a quick run down. All of a sudden there may be:

- Pressure to perform academically.
- Financial stress.
- Conflict with parents.
- Physical and/or mental exhaustion.
- Not getting along with friends.
- Bullying; online or in person.
- Hormonal and body changes.
- Break-ups, make-ups, and all that in between.

Can you relate to any of these? Circle the ones that you connect with. Are there are others?

_____

_____

For the first time in your life you may be experiencing a whole new set of hardships. That is not to say that everyone has a "happy" childhood, but when you reach your teens and early 20s, you are likely encountering a whole new ballgame in terms of relational dynamics, academic pressures, and personal emotions. Everything can feel heightened at this age—love can feel fantastic, disappointment can feel bitter, and frustration can feel like agony. Emotions feel extreme sometimes and when you are living in that moment of intensity, it can feel all-consuming. Sometimes these feelings can feel amazing and other times they can feel completely crippling. How do you work through those emotions when it feels like they will take you over?

When these feelings become so powerful it is important for us to step back and ask ourselves what is going on. If we can understand *why* we are feeling the way we do, we can begin to sift through our emotions. Sometimes the answer is obvious (your partner broke up with you, so you feel sad) but sometimes it can be much more complicated (you got into your dream school, but you don't feel excited—why is that?). Emotions are complex and we can often feel multiple emotions at once. This can be confusing for us because we are subliminally told that we cannot feel mixed emotions at once (also known as ambivalence). But we certainly can. For example, maybe you really like your roommate but you also feel claustrophobic when she's around. Or you're glad you won the soccer game but you feel mad at yourself that you didn't score a goal. These are what we call paradoxical emotional experiences. As humans we are multifaceted in our emotional abilities and we can feel conflicting emotions at the same time. Once we know this, our emotions might not feel so unsettling to us.

Instead of getting frustrated at ourselves for not feeling how we think we "should," we can begin to accept ourselves unconditionally for the feelings that we do have. Many of us judge ourselves harshly for not feeling a certain way. We may get mad at ourselves for not laughing more or having more fun. We may feel disappointed in ourselves that we feel sad or worried when we "should" be happy. We can really beat ourselves up if we're not careful. We might start to compare ourselves to others, saying that someone else is "better looking," "smarter," or "more talented" than we are. But instead of competing with others, we can treat ourselves with unconditional acceptance and love. We can welcome our feelings—be they positive or negative—and we can give ourselves space to feel how we need to feel. We can try to let go of the mental rankings of how we compare to others, and instead, we can just focus on how we can be healthy individuals. You will hear me say it throughout the book but it is so important that you know that you are enough just as you are.

You are welcomed, wanted, and loved no matter what.

You are deserving of care, no matter how you feel. You are lovable when you're angry, helpless, and lonely—not just when you happy and smiling.

This mentality needs to start with you. You need to believe these good things about yourself. I can tell you, your friends and family can tell you—anyone can tell you—but if you don't believe it, your emotions may try to wreak havoc on you. They may try to tell you that you are worthless, that you don't matter, or that you're a failure.

These messages can be pretty powerful if you aren't equipped to say otherwise. And while I hope that you have someone in your corner to tell you how much you matter, ultimately you have to believe that yourself.

What are three kind things you can say about yourself?

1. _____

2. _____

3. _____

Emotions are not something to be afraid of. They are powerful indicators of how we are feeling and they can be our guide if we are willing to listen. Now I'm not saying you should completely ignore logic and follow your feelings blindly. We need to have that head-heart balance to make the most informed decisions possible. But emotions can be our gut's way of telling us how to protect ourselves; this is why we often have a physical reaction when we are having an emotional experience. What could some of these be?

- Dry mouth when getting ready to give a speech in class.
- Queasy stomach when you see a scary movie.
- Shaky hands when you get a job offer.
- A hot face when getting in a fight with your parent.
- Sweaty palms when going on a first date.

You can see how the body reacts differently for different emotions. These are clues that signal how we are feeling and the body wants us to pay attention. Sometimes these reactions may feel out of proportion and the good news is that there are many ways to get help if it bothers you. Sometimes we can feel embarrassed if we feel our emotions are too obvious, like blushing when a crush walks by or not being able to speak during an interview. While there are many ways to remedy this depending on what you're experiencing, it is important to know that everyone has emotional reactions sometimes. We all have times that we respond in ways that may feel embarrassing and that's okay.

We are human beings with physical bodies and we have all felt frustrated before by our bodies' "give aways." This might include throwing up because we feel so nervous for a test or crying in front of others because we didn't make the volleyball team. When this happens to you, don't be afraid to own your experience. So long as your emotions do not physically or emotionally hurt other people, you are entitled to feel how you feel. You don't ever need to apologize for that. We can also hope that the people around us will have compassion towards us, especially if we feel humiliated by our emotional reaction. In fact, people often grow closer after an emotionally vulnerable experience together. Did you ever feel more connected to someone after they shared a personal experience with you?

And if someone makes fun of you or teases you because of how you reacted, just know that they likely have a lot of unprocessed emotions, pain, and insecurity that they unfortunately acted out on you. While it is so easy to take it personally, know that the problem lies within them. The fact that they would take advantage of another person's vulnerability signifies their own heartache.

While we can have momentary reactions, the body can also send us clues that can feel longer lasting. Or we may have thoughts that we haven't had before but are now more constant. Perhaps you can identify with some of the following or you have noticed some of these changes within others around you.

Sleep: In the past few weeks, you are sleeping much more than usual or you can hardly sleep at all.

Interests: You're no longer interested in the hobbies you used to enjoy. You've stopped going to practice and you no longer feel excited by the idea of participating in what you once loved. This may be piano, art, dance—whatever you like.

Guilty: You have a nagging feeling that you did something wrong and you can't shake it. You feel responsible for something "bad" that has happened.

Energy: You feel like you have no energy to accomplish the tasks you need to complete or you have so much energy you can hardly sit still.

Concentration: You have an inability to focus; no matter how hard you try. It feels impossible to get your homework and assignments done.

Appetite: You can't get enough to eat or you hardly want to eat. You've gained or lost more than 5% of your body weight in the past two weeks.

Thoughts about Harm: You are having thoughts of hurting yourself or others. You might be thinking about a plan to carry out this harm.

Can you identify with any of these feelings or physical experiences? Circle any that you have experienced consistently for the past two weeks.

Again, this is not meant as a diagnostic tool but instead, use this is a guide to help you identify if something feels a little "different" or "off." Sometimes we don't notice if change is happening until it suddenly feels overwhelming. This list is meant to help give you some clues for any small changes you may be experiencing. In this next chapter we'll break down what some of these changes may mean.

Naming It

By now you've heard the terms "depression" and "anxiety" but you may be unsure of what they actually mean. I'm going to cover some of the most commonly occurring mental health conditions that adolescents and young adults experience. This is certainly not a comprehensive review of every diagnosis. I wanted to cover some of the more common experiences that you or someone you know may relate to presently. A few key notes before we start. You'll notice that I try to be very conscientious about using the term disorder. In the Diagnostic and Statistical Manual—5 (DSM-V), most of these experiences are penned as disorders[8]. They are called disorders because they are related to someone's impairment in functioning— whether that relates to work, school, relationships, etc. While this may be the proper terminology, I want to make sure that you know that having a "disorder" does not mean that someone cannot still achieve their full potential. While a disorder means that someone may have a harder time in different capacities, we should never judge someone's abilities just because they have a diagnosable condition.

As you are reading this chapter, the big question you may have is: *"But why? Why me? Why them? This feels so unfair. I don't understand why this is happening."* These are questions that everyone asks—including scientists. When someone has a challenge with their mental health, whether they feel so sad that they can't get out of bed, or they are so worried that they experience a panic attack, we always want to understand what is going on. The answer is complicated, and scientists and clinicians are working hard every day to understand these conditions even more.

In a nutshell, mental health conditions are a mix of our biology and our environment. Some people may have a greater genetic likelihood to experience different disorders. This means that their genes, or their DNA, may carry traits that may make them more likely to develop certain characteristics, like anxiety or depression, for instance. Other people may live through such challenging life experiences and may react to those traumas in many ways, including feeling loneliness, anger, and/or potentially the desire to self-harm. And sometimes it is a mix. A person may have a family history with mental health challenges and then becomes triggered by an upsetting life event. As a result they may potentially develop something like Posttraumatic Stress Disorder (PTSD) or an eating disorder. All of these different situations do not equate to destiny, though. Just because you have a family member who has been unwell or you have lived through hardship does not mean that you are bound to develop a disorder. Chances are, you are more resilient than you realize. However, if you are going through a hard time and you are diagnosed with a disorder, it does not mean you are "flawed" or "broken." The best thing you can do is inform yourself and become educated on the steps you need to take in order to feel like your best self.

A final note to be cautious of before you read this chapter: doctors will often joke about "medical student syndrome," because when they are learning about every possible disease they might encounter, they start to fear that they in fact have many of the diseases they are learning about. I experienced something similar when I began my doctoral program—I could identify more than five disorders that I surely had. The same applied to the people around me; I started to speculate what conditions they might have as well. It is very easy to read a list of symptoms and believe that we fit the bill; but it's not that simple. This information that I'm about to provide is really so that you can be mindful and informed rather than to self-diagnose yourself or someone else. If you suspect that you may be experiencing one or more of these conditions, I highly encourage you to visit a therapist and/or a doctor who can help you take the next best steps. And if you have a friend that you are concerned about, that is not to say that you shouldn't still approach them because you are unsure if they have a diagnosable condition. You can still express caring without coming off like a doctor who has already diagnosed them.

If you are in fact diagnosed with a disorder or condition or you know someone who is, remember that these "labels" do not define you or anyone. We never say that someone is schizophrenic, autistic, or anorexic. We never label anyone by their disorder. Instead, they are a person who has schizophrenia, autism, and/or anorexia. These words do not put us in boxes and they do not make us a certain "type" of person. The descriptions of these experiences are meant to give us a framework to help us understand what someone may be going through but we should never assume how someone is feeling. Every person has the right to their minds, emotions, and bodies and it is up to each of us to decide how we feel about our mental health. For some, learning about diagnosable conditions can feel empowering, containing, or upsetting. Every reaction is acceptable and understandable. Check in with yourself as you read this chapter and reach out to a trusted person if you are feeling scared, nervous, or overwhelmed.

If you'd like to learn more about any of the following disorders, you can go to the resources section at the back of the book. This will guide you to specific websites that focus on certain disorders.

Anxiety Disorders

Let's start with the most common mental health concern: **Anxiety.** 25% of adolescents experience it and 40 million adults over the age of 18 experience anxiety. 75% of those living with anxiety have their first episode by age 22. Some symptoms of **Generalized Anxiety** may include:

- Excessive worry or fear occurring more days than not and this worrying feels out of control.
- Feeling restless, on edge, irritable.
- Exhaustion and/or fatigue.
- Trouble concentrating on tasks.
- Body tensing, sweaty palms, rapid heart rate, tightness in chest.
- Trouble sleeping.

Almost all of us have experienced some of these symptoms at some point—especially when something important was happening in our lives like taking the SAT or singing in the school talent show. However, when the worry is happening for more than six months and feels almost constant, that may be a clue that the anxious thoughts are more far-reaching; they are impacting your daily living.

There is a big difference between anxiety and everyday worrying. We all need a little bit of stress in our lives to perform at our highest standard. When we don't care at all, our performance tends to suffer. When we care too much, we are crippled, and as a result, we are less effective. Ideally, we have that sweet spot where we care enough to do well—this means that there is just a little bit of nervousness attached.[9] This is that feeling of butterflies in your stomach before the prom or your voice shaking a little at first when you start your class presentation—it means that you care. But when the stress becomes too much—to the point where are handicapped in a way (trouble speaking, body feels out of control, etc.) and this feeling is upsetting, it can be a sign of Generalized Anxiety, especially if this sense of concern happens every day on a regular basis.

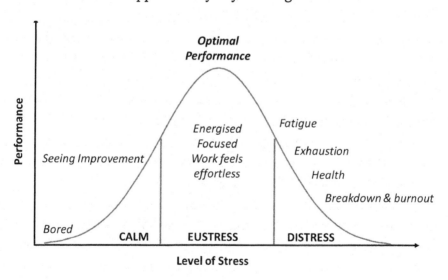

Image credit to Jing Teak Ong

Circle on the chart *how you usually feel when it comes time for a performance (this includes activities like a basketball game, a dance performance, a math test—any time you are expected to "perform well" in your life).*

How do you respond to stress?

_____

_____

Do you feel like you ever experience physical symptoms of anxiety? If so, how often do you have a physical reaction?

_____

_____

Sometimes anxiety can be experienced very somatically (meaning the body responds with a physical feeling and/or symptoms), and we see this most often with **Panic Attacks**. In a given year, 2-3% of adults will experience a panic attack and while they can happen in adolescents and children, they are less common. Symptoms might include a pounding heart, sweating, trembling or shaking, shortness of breath, a feeling of choking, chest pain, nausea, feeling dizzy, chills or heat sensations, and potentially feeling like one is dying or losing control of their body. It can be a very scary experience while one is actively feeling the symptoms of a panic attack. The best thing you can do is to take slow, deep breaths and to sit or lay down in a quiet space. Other people feel better when they have someone talking them through the experience and sitting beside them. Each person is different with what they need in that moment.

There are many different conditions that fall under the anxiety umbrella. Some people may experience **Social Anxiety,** which is when you experience anxiety during certain social situations, like a party with new people, a job interview, or when you have to perform. You may be worried about how people will judge you and you may actually avoid the situation so that you won't have to experience the anxious feelings. The avoidance might make you feel upset because you feel like you are missing out (FOMO), but you also hate how uncomfortable you feel when you're in that certain social setting.

Do you ever get nervous when you're in certain social situations? If so, which ones?

_____

_____

Other people may have a **Specific Phobia.** This may be when a certain object or situation provokes immense fear. A person with a phobia is likely to try to flee to avoid the thing or object they fear. This fear is out of proportion to the actual danger posed by the object or situation but the person feels incredibly frightened nonetheless. This is often a longstanding fear that lasts at least longer than six months.

I believe in transparency in this book so I'll take this opportunity to disclose my own experience with a phobia. For as long as I can remember, I have been incredibly afraid of throwing up—either when someone else does it or I do it, I nearly have a panic attack because I become so afraid. This is such a powerful reaction that I have literally run in the opposite direction when I see someone getting sick. I find this so upsetting because I want to support my friend who is sick but my body literally seizes me and catapults me away from the retching. Now if you have not experienced a phobia before, it can almost seem laughable how afraid someone gets when provoked by their phobia. But if you have experienced a phobia—perhaps you're afraid of snakes, planes, spiders, blood, or needles, for example—which are some of the more common ones, then you know just how powerful the phobia can be. You will avoid it at all costs. Depending on the phobia, this fear can be very inhibiting for people and can hold them back in various ways. Thankfully, this is a highly treatable condition and with **Exposure and Response Prevention therapy**, it can often be improved. In Exposure and Response Prevention therapy, the therapist exposes the client to their feared item or situation at gradual levels of intensity to help the person face what scares them. As they progress through the therapy, they begin to see that their fear is out of proportion to the direct threat. It's hard to get people to start this kind of therapy (because they are deathly afraid of even looking at the feared situation or object!) but if they can give the therapy an honest effort, it is often successful.

Do you have any specific phobias? If so, would you be willing to try something like Exposure and Response Prevention therapy?

_____

_____

Another condition that young adults may experience is **Separation Anxiety**. Such anxiety often arises in this age group sometimes because there are many transitions occurring in a young adult's life, including going to college. Some high school students can't wait to leave the nest and others are dreading going away to school. Here are some of the symptoms that you or someone you know may be experiencing:

- Recurrent and intense distress when thinking about leaving the home or being away from important people in your life.
- A persistent fear about you or a loved one experiencing an illness, injury, disaster, or death that could lead to separation.
- Reluctance or refusal to leave the home, go to work/school, or elsewhere because of fear of separation.
- Reluctance or refusal to sleep away from the home or away from loved one.
- Nightmares involving separation with a loved one.
- Physical symptoms including headaches, stomachaches, nausea, and/or vomiting when anticipating or currently separated from loved one.

If you have yet to leave the home, how do you feel about moving out someday? If you have moved out, how was that experience for you? Were you lonely or was it a smooth transition?

People may also experience what is called **Agoraphobia**, or a fear of being in public places. This may include an avoidance of public transportation (buses, planes, cars, etc.) and/or a dislike of being in open spaces (parking lots, walking paths, parks, etc.) or even enclosed, public spaces (movie theaters, malls, elevators, etc.). There may be a fear of standing in a crowd or being outside of the home alone. About 1.7% of teens and adults have this condition and females are twice as likely as males to experience it.

Of the described Anxiety conditions, do you identify with any symptoms? If so, which ones?

If you did identify with any of the symptoms, are any of them upsetting to you?

If you feel upset by any of these potential symptoms, who is a safe person that you can talk about it with?

Obsessive-Compulsive and Related Disorders

While **Obsessive-Compulsive Disorder (OCD)** is an anxious condition, it is different than the previously mentioned experiences because it includes repetitive behaviors. About 1.2% of the population has OCD symptoms with females affected at a slightly higher rate in adulthood. However, during childhood, boys are more likely to experience the condition. OCD has two parts: obsessions *and* compulsions. Obsessions are persistent thoughts, urges, or images that are intrusive and unwanted; they cause the person to feel worried or upset. The person may try to suppress or stop the thoughts by carrying out a compulsion, or a repetitive behavior, to try and make the thought go away. This might include washing hands, checking objects, or counting in a ritualistic way. The person feels like they have to carry out these behaviors or something bad might happen. These behaviors are very time consuming (taking more than an hour per day) and the person feels like they are not able to do as well in school or work because of their obsessions and compulsions.

Another experience that about 2.5% of the population experiences is **Body Dysmorphic Disorder**. This is when someone is obsessed with one or more "flaws" in their physical appearance that no one else would notice. The person has repetitive behaviors like checking the mirror, spending hours getting ready, or comparing their appearance to others.

How do you feel about your body?

_____

_____

If you could change something about your body, would you?

_____

_____

Do you feel like you compare your body to others? _____ Yes _____ No

One last set of conditions that is less common but I have seen in clinical practice is what is called **Trichotillomania**, or **Hair-Pulling**. This is when a person pulls out their hair so that there is hair loss, even though they make repeated attempts to stop doing so. A similar condition is **Excoriation**, or **Skin-Picking**. This is when a person picks at their skin to the point when there are skin lesions and scars, even though the person has tried to stop picking their skin. Both conditions occur in about 1-2% of the population. I think it is important to talk about both of these because you may have met someone with one or both of these conditions, or you yourself may experience it, and unfortunately there is not much education or awareness about what these conditions entail. These can be very challenging conditions and it is so important that we not judge others or make fun of them for what they are going through, particularly if you notice things like hair loss or red skin. Even though someone may look different, we have to remember not to judge them—we are not walking in their shoes. Instead, we can choose to be compassionate with one another and accept each other wholeheartedly.

Of the described Obsessive Compulsive conditions, do you identify with any symptoms? If so, which ones?

_____

_____

If you did identify with any of the symptoms, are any of them upsetting to you?

_____

_____

If you feel upset by any of these potential symptoms, who is a safe person that you can talk about it with?

_____

Trauma and Stressor Related Disorders

While there are quite a few diagnoses within this heading, I think the main one to note is **Posttraumatic Stress Disorder (PTSD).** This is when a person either directly experiences a traumatic event or when they witness a traumatic event happening to someone else. Trauma can vary—it may include death, sickness, or anything that one finds disturbing. What ultimately matters is whether or not the person felt traumatized by the experience. Every person's level of tolerance is different. For example, Sarah may feel traumatized by her family cat's death, but her brother, John, did not feel like it was a big deal. He was sad that his cat died, but he was not traumatized by it. Trauma is highly personal. We all have different things that upset us in varying degrees. Furthermore, just because someone experiences trauma, it does not mean they will develop PTSD. We all have different resources and strengths and this can help us persevere. But sometimes that trauma may be so horrific or a person may have multiple tragedies that occur simultaneously or continuously that the trauma build-up is too much.

What are the symptoms of PTSD? It may include recurrent and distressing memories, frequent dreams about the traumatic incident, dissociative reactions (where one feels like they are out of their body, re-experiencing the trauma once more), and/or intense and prolong psychological distress when one feels "triggered" by symbols or cues that remind the person of the traumatic experience.

I do not want to leave you feeling triggered by reading about trauma. If a significant memory or memories are coming to mind as you're reading this section, I strongly recommend seeking professional help. PTSD can be treated and even though it may seem counterintuitive, talking about it with a professional can really help heal the pain. A therapist can guide you in retelling your story and re-framing it in such a way that you can live your life feeling more integrated and whole. We all have bad things happen in our lives but no person should be victim to suffering on a daily basis. You do not have to be a prisoner to your trauma—trust that someone will value your story and will help you find peace. And if it feels too soon to talk about any trauma that you have experienced in your life, that is okay, too. A good therapist should never force someone to talk about painful experiences until the client is ready. Remember that you can always go at your own pace. You are the owner of your life story and the only person that can tell it is you.

If it would help you to write about the thoughts coming to mind right now, including any feelings or memories that are coming to mind, here is a space for you to do so:

_____

_____

_____

_____

If you felt upset learning about PTSD, who is a safe person that you can talk about it with?

Depressive and Bipolar Disorders

It's important to spend time talking about depression because some young adults actively experience it but they may not understand it fully. Our society does not always make it "okay" or even "safe" to feel sad, and I want to provide a space here to say that it's okay to not feel okay. There are all times when we feel hopeless, helpless, and down. And while we need to allow ourselves to feel how we truly feel, there are also many things we can do to feel better (which I will cover in just a bit). But with depression, there is a difference between "having the blues" and what is called **Major Depressive Disorder (MDD).** No matter how hard you try to "shake it off" or "pick yourself up," you feel like you just can't when it comes to Major Depression. And while everything on the surface of your life may seem fine, and some may even say, "you have no reason to be sad," depression does not discriminate. Sometimes you may just have this deep sadness that you feel like you're drowning in. So what might MDD include? Here are some of the potential symptoms:

- Feeling sad, empty, or hopeless, most of the day, nearly every day, for at least two weeks. For children and teens it could include irritability.
- Much less interest in activities or hobbies that used to bring you joy.
- Significant weight loss not due to dieting (change of more than 5% of body weight in a month).
- Getting too much sleep or not enough nearly every day.
- Others have noticed that you move more slowly.
- Feeling fatigued and having a loss of energy.
- Feeling worthless and/or experiencing a large amount of guilt.

- Trouble concentrating, feeling indecisive.
- Thoughts of death, potentially thinking about suicide.

Perhaps you might be identifying with some of these symptoms. That would not be too surprising as 12.5% of the population between the ages of 12 and 17 experiences an episode of Major Depressive Disorder in a given year. Within this age bracket, 19.5% of girls experience MDD in a year while 5.8% of boys do as well.[10] Depression is even more prevalent in college, with 36.4% of students saying that they have experienced depressive symptoms. In fact, depression is the number one reason that students drop out of college.[11] The good news is that depression can be very treatable and the experience does not have to last forever. We will talk in the coming chapters about what you can do to feel better or how you can help if you see someone else struggling.

Another condition within this category is called **Bipolar Disorder**. You may have heard people use this word to describe someone whose personality seems to change frequently, just like Katy Perry's "Hot and Cold" song. However, Bipolar Disorder has a much more specific definition that may be different than what you thought. The condition includes two experiences: a Major Depressive Episode (as described above) and a Manic Episode. What is mania? It is a time when a person might experience some or all of the following:

- Distinct periods of time when a person has an unusual amount of elevated or expansive energy. Feeling irritable and/or having excessive goal-directed behavior.
- Becoming overly involved in activities.
- Inflated self-esteem.
- Decreased need for sleep—feeling rested after three hours of sleep. Staying awake for days on end.
- More talkative than usual.
- Racing thoughts, easily distracted.

There are different levels of mania; a manic episode is more intense than what is called a hypomanic episode. A manic episode will often result in someone being hospitalized while a hypomanic episode is less intense. Bipolar disorder is seen in about .6% of the population and it does have a genetic heritability component. It is much less common than Major Depression Disorder, but it's still important to know the signs since it often emerges in young adulthood. Bipolar disorder is treated with medication and many people go on to lead incredibly successful lives.

In fact, one of my speaking mentors, Ross Szabo, lives with Bipolar Disorder. His diagnosis is a side note though when you consider his incredible accolades. He has had the opportunity to travel the country speaking about mental health, he has worked with the Clinton family to promote national mental health curriculum (which he created), and he has traveled to Africa to work with the Peace Corps. That's a pretty incredible life! The fact that he can do all these things and more is a reminder that a diagnosis like Bipolar disorder does not have to define your life. Ross is a great example of that.

Of the described Depressive conditions, do you identify with any symptoms? If so, which ones?

_____

_____

If you did identify with any of the symptoms, are any of them upsetting to you?

_____

_____

If you feel upset by any of these potential symptoms, who is a safe person that you can talk about it with?

Schizophrenia

I would be remiss if I did not cover **Schizophrenia**. This word is definitely a "Voldemort" word and people avoid having conversations about what it means when a person is living with schizophrenia. Yet we see the symptoms of schizophrenia quite often; we see it on our streets as some people who are without homes live with it. Many of us have family members or friends who have been diagnosed with it. I think it is especially important to talk about schizophrenia with young adults because it is typically diagnosed between the late teens and mid 30s. While rare with 0.3-0.7% of the population being diagnosed with schizophrenia, it is still important to learn about it so that we can approach those who are struggling with kindness.

Many of us feel fearful or avoidant when we see someone with schizophrenia, but it is important to know that more often than not, the person is not dangerous or someone to be fearful of. That is not to say that you should not be cognizant around the person (especially if that is what your gut is telling you to do), but generally, people with schizophrenia are not violent, especially towards others. They are people with feelings and lived experiences, just like you and me.

What are some of the signs of schizophrenia? You may think of "positive symptoms," or symptoms that are beyond what is expected of typical behavior. Such symptoms may include delusions, which are false beliefs that the person feels are true. For instance, a person experiencing delusions might believe that he or she is famous, being followed, or that aliens are invading earth. Someone suffering from schizophrenia might also have hallucinations, which are sensory experiences that the person experiences when there is actually nothing there. For example, he or she might see bugs on the wall, they may hear a voice, or they may even smell or hear things that are not actually there. The person will likely also have "negative symptoms," which means that they are lacking the behaviors or responses that would be expected in typical behavior. For example, the person might display a lack of emotion, stiff body movement, or have trouble speaking.

Schizophrenia can include episodes of psychosis (where the person experiences hallucinations and/or delusions). However, people with schizophrenia can also enter into remission and not experience the positive symptoms that were previously described. This is a condition where medication is almost always required to help reduce symptoms. Having a supportive family can make all the difference for someone living with schizophrenia, and if you have a family member or friend who is struggling with schizophrenia, the best thing you can do is be there for that person rather than turn away. It should be noted that schizophrenia is a complex diagnosis and if you want to learn more about this particular disorder, I encourage you to seek resources that specifically focuses on schizophrenia education.

Thankfully the perspective on schizophrenia is shifting. Our society used to believe that people diagnosed with schizophrenia were bound to live a life in and out of hospitals and there wasn't much hope. Now we know that when a person receives resources and support and is consistent with their treatment, they can still accomplish a great deal and have a healthy and happy life.

What feelings came up for you as you were reading about schizophrenia?

_____

_____

Do you know anyone who has experienced schizophrenia? How has your experience been with that person?

_____

_____

Feeding and Eating Disorders

Eating and food can bring about a challenge that just about everybody faces at some point. We live in a country where we are often not enough as we are. We are not thin enough, curvy enough, tall enough, short enough, strong enough, or toned enough. It can feel like there is a new expectation lurking around every corner, no matter how hard you try. And whether or not you buy into the criticism, it is not hard to start placing those harsh standards on yourself. Rather than embrace our bodies, we often turn to food as an unhealthy way to cope. We may start eating too much or not enough as a way to punish our bodies and suppress our feelings.

In fact, 50% of teenage girls and 30% of teenage boys have used unhealthy methods to manage their weight. This includes skipping meals, fasting, smoking cigarettes, vomiting, and/or taking laxatives.[12] This is happening at younger and younger ages, too. 46% of 9 to 11 year-olds are "sometimes" or "often" on diets. Sometimes these unhealthy approaches to weight can create life-threatening risks. In fact, someone dies from an eating disorder every hour.[13] I don't mean for this to scare you, but I think it's important to be knowledgeable about what these eating conditions include so that you can be preventative if possible.

What is especially hard about eating disorders is that there is sometimes what is called a "comorbid diagnosis" that goes hand and hand with the eating disorder. This means that the person has not only one diagnosable condition, but two or more. This phenomenon can happen with other conditions, such as having a substance use disorder and major depressive disorder, but it is particularly prevalent with eating disorders. 33-55% of those living with anorexia, bulimia, or binge-eating also have a mood disorder, like major depression. Someone with anorexia, bulimia, or binge-eating may also experience some form of anxiety, like OCD or social anxiety—indeed this happens 50% of the time.[14]

The first condition occurring in about 1% to 4.2% of women is **Anorexia Nervosa.**[15] While men experience anorexia, it currently occurs at a 10:1 female-to-male ratio. Believe it or not, anorexia has the highest fatality rate of any mental health condition. In fact, 4% of people diagnosed die from complications and 1 in 5 anorexia deaths is by suicide.[16][17] What is especially sad is that only a third of people with anorexia get the help that they need.[18]

What exactly is anorexia? It is a condition where a restricts their food so much that their weight drops to a significantly low amount, given that person's height, sex, and age. The person is extremely afraid of gaining weight and/or becoming fat and they see themselves as large, even if they are of normal or even low weight. The person will obsess about their food intake and may also focus on exercise, calories, and their physical appearance.

Another condition that is based on food intake and body image is **Bulimia Nervosa.** This is when the person will binge-eat, or consume a large amount of food in a single sitting, and then the person will purge the food to avoid weight gain. This may include vomiting, using laxatives, diuretics, excessive exercise, or fasting. When the person is binge eating they will feel out of control and purging is an attempt to regain some of that control. This experience occurs for about 4% of women at some point in their lives in the United States.[19] However, the prevalence rate is highest for girls who are in their older adolescence and young adulthood. Only 6% of people living with bulimia obtain treatment, even less than the percentage of people with anorexia who seek treatment.

Another less well-known but just as challenging eating condition is **Binge-Eating.** This is similar to bulimia in terms of the binge eating but it does not include purging. The person feels out of control when they are eating excessive amounts in a sitting and they will feel uncomfortably full after the eating session. They may feel embarrassed by their behavior and even feel disgusted, depressed, or guilty afterward. This occurs about once a week on average for a person living with binge-eating disorder. And while approximately 2.8% of Americans live with this diagnosis, there are many outlets of support for this community. In particular, groups like Overeaters Anonymous provide members with a safe space to process the emotional triggers that prompt their overeating.

We have a long way to go when it comes to loving our bodies. In any given day, 25% of Americans are actively dieting. It's even worse for college students. 91% of college women say they have tried to control their weight by restricting their calories.[20] Learning to love ourselves is a lifelong journey and it's normal that you may feel frustrated with your body at times as it grows and changes. If you can choose to accept your body, and trust that someone else will as well, you are on the path to wellness. Your body will thank you for it!

Of the previously discussed Eating conditions, do you identify with any of the symptoms that were described? If so, which ones?

_____

_____

Do you know anyone who is struggling with their eating? Have you been able to express your concern for them?

_____

_____

If you feel upset by any of these potential symptoms, who is a safe person that you can talk about it with?

_____

Substance-Related and Addictive Disorders

Sometimes people may try to cope with their stress or sadness by controlling their food intake (as mentioned above) while others may cope by using alcohol or other drugs. While covering all of the various drugs that frequently used would be beyond the scope of this book, it is important to understand what the signs of addiction are so that you or someone you love can start to get some help. No one should have to live with addiction. The good news is that it's so much better to catch this habit at a younger age because the body and brain are not as enmeshed in the addiction and it is easier to break the cycle.

It's not surprising that people turn to drugs or alcohol as a way to deal with their problems. It numbs the pain and it can make you feel good for a short amount of time. The problem though is that we begin depending on this to remedy when we feel down, and sooner or later, we need the substance just to feel *okay*. The scary part about this is that the younger a person is when they start drinking, the more likely they are to become addicted. In fact, a person who starts drinking between the ages of 11 and 14 has a 16% of chance of becoming an alcoholic 10 years later while someone who waits until they are 19 or older to start drinking has a 1% of chance of the same outcome.[21]

There are certain risk factors that can make someone more susceptible to developing a substance use disorder. Risk factors include: a family history of addiction, being male (although the progression of addictive disorders develops more quickly in females), having another mental health disorder (comorbidity), peer pressure, and lack of family involvement, just to name a few.[22] Addiction is particularly prevalent in members of the LGBTQ community. 20-30% of people within this population abuse substances and 25% abuse alcohol.[23]

While there are separate categories depending on the substance, I think it is important to note some general signs that you or someone you know may be struggling with substance abuse. Here is what to look out for over a 12-month period:

- Taking the substance in large amounts or over a longer period of time than initially planned. Developing a tolerance which then requires ingesting more of the substance to feel the effects.
- Experiencing strong desires or unsuccessful attempts to cut back on usage.
- Needing to take time to recover from the effects of the substance (hangover). Withdrawal symptoms occur when no longer taking the substance.
- Experiencing cravings or strong urges to use the substance.
- Being unable to accomplish obligations at school, work, or home due to substance use.
- Continuing to use the drug even though it negatively impacts relationships.
- Giving up hobbies, social, work, or family activities due to substance use.
- Continuing to use the substance, despite dangerous and life-threatening circumstances, like driving under the influence.

There are also some other signs that you might notice in someone suffering from addiction, including a sudden decline in performance at school, in extracurricular activities, or at work, unexplained laughter, poor hygiene, a sudden increase in secrecy, increased tiredness, and/or blood shot eyes. It's important to be aware of these signs because alcohol and substance abuse is not altogether uncommon. Alcohol is the most commonly used substance of choice with 20% of 12th graders binge drinking. Nearly 40% report using alcohol in the last month. Marijuana is also frequently used with 20% of teens saying that they have used it in the past month. In addition, 1 in 5 teens abuse prescription medications.[24]

We need to be just as mindful in college. Those who are enrolled in a full-time college program are twice as likely to abuse drugs and alcohol than those who don't attend college. Four out of five college students drink with nearly half of those students saying that they binge drink (when a man consumes 5 or more drinks or a woman consumes 4 or more drinks within a 2-hour time span).[25] What's more, about 30% of students use drugs like non-prescribed Adderall, Ritalin, or Vyvance as "study aids" to help them meet their academic demands.[26] This is especially dangerous because these drugs can lead to unhealthy weight loss, irritability, trouble sleeping, restlessness, and even cardiac issues.[27]

People often get defensive when they learn about substance use. "I don't have a problem—how dare you!" "It's not that big of a deal—everyone does it." "I'm not addicted because I can stop when I want." Defensiveness is one of the biggest signs that someone is in denial about their actual use of substances. So if you were reading the list above and identifying with quite a few, maybe it's time to take an honest look at how you're doing. There is nothing wrong with reaching out for help. While it can be very hard to create new and more adaptive ways of coping, it will ultimately prolong your life and increase the fulfillment that you get out of it.

Do you identify with any of the symptoms that were described above? If so, which ones?

_____

_____

If you did identify with any of the symptoms, are any of them upsetting to you? Did you feel yourself getting defensive at all?

_____

_____

Do you know anyone who is struggling with substance use? Have you been able to express your concern for them?

_____

_____

If you feel upset by any of these potential symptoms, who is a safe person that you can talk about it with?

_____

It can be hard to read about these signs. It is normal for young adults to experiment, and one of the ways this may happen is by trying alcohol or other substances. And while I am not endorsing this if you are under age, I will say that if you are going to try something, please do so safely. Be around people that you know and trust. You don't need to impress anyone. While we all have experimented at some point in our lives (whether that is sky diving, trying sushi, or having a beer—hey, it's different for everyone), you have to respect your body and listen to your limits.

Neurodevelopmental Disorders

Some conditions are more likely to be diagnosed in childhood and you may be more familiar with the following conditions. Chances are you've had a classmate, sibling, or friend who has lived with one of the following conditions. Even if you already know a little bit about these experiences, it's still important to learn more. I think we owe it to the people around us who have lived with these disorders to learn about and appreciate their experiences. They deserve respect, compassion, and understanding—just like anyone else. For example, you may know someone who has **Autism Spectrum Disorder**. It is expected that 2 million people in the US live with autism, with boys being 4-5 times more likely to develop autism than girls. Therefore, about 1 in 68 children are diagnosed with autism.[28] Autism has a great deal of variance with a wide range of symptoms and expressions (hence it is on a spectrum). But what are some common signs in teens and young adults?

- Trouble socializing and empathizing with others.
- Struggling to maintain friendships, particularly in group settings.
- Hard time understanding body language, facial expressions, and gestures.
- Difficulty making eye contact.
- Obsessions with rigid routines.

Just because someone has autism, it does not mean that you cannot be friends or that they don't want to get to know you. In fact, people living with autism often have some of the most incredible gifts that are so worth getting to know. Sometimes they are brilliant in a particular dimension, like playing a musical instrument or completing math calculations. People with such skills are called savants. But other times they may be masters with puzzles or just incredibly friendly. I'll never forget the day that I volunteered at Special Olympics with my mom in National Charity League. I didn't want to volunteer that Saturday morning but my mom told me it would be fun so I should come along. Sure enough, I met a boy there who had autism and he was preparing for his race. He hugged each of the volunteers at least five times that day—myself included. He didn't win his race but he was the happiest kid I've ever met! We all were smiling so much just being around him. Now that is a gift. If I hadn't shown up that day, I would have missed out on the opportunity to meet an incredible person.

It's easy to shy away from people who do things differently than us. We may feel scared or uncomfortable because we don't know how to react. But just remember, we are all just people trying to get by in the world. If you're willing to laugh at yourself, ask questions, and just be kind to others, you will be an amazing force for good. Don't worry if you're awkward or nervous when you meet someone with autism, or any other condition for that matter. What's important is that you don't avoid people because they're different than you. Take the time to get to know them because chances are, you will learn something from them and you may even make a new friend. And regardless, it always feels better to know that you treated someone with kindness rather than cruelty.

Do you know anyone who has autism? How did or do you treat them?

Another experience within this category is **Attention-Deficit/ Hyperactivity Disorder (ADHD).** ADHD is fairly common with 11% of children between the ages of 14 and 17 being diagnosed with this at some point in their lives.[29] Boys are three times more likely to have ADHD (13.2%) than girls (5.6%).[30] And contrary to popular opinion, ADHD does not go away during adolescence. Adults live with ADHD, although it often goes undiagnosed because only recently has the condition gained more attention.

When we hear about ADHD, we often think about the hyperactivity component. A diagnosis of ADHD involves symptoms that last for at least six months and can include fidgeting, inability to remain seated, running/climbing at inappropriate times, inability to be quiet/talks excessively, interrupting others, and/or having difficulty waiting their turn. However, the inattention part of ADHD is often less noticed by parents and teachers and this may be why girls are diagnosed less often. These symptoms include making careless mistakes on schoolwork, trouble maintaining focus during play or conversations, daydreaming when spoken to, inability to follow instructions, trouble organizing, procrastinating on projects that take a lot of time, losing things, and being forgetful with important deadlines.

Now of course, each of us can think of examples when we have been both hyperactive and inattentive. If you ask me, I think our cell phones have definitely contributed to the latter. But just because you relate to some of the symptoms, it does not mean that you have ADHD. Remember, in order to receive a diagnosis you need to not only meet the criteria for symptoms, you also need to be impaired by the condition. With this in mind, if you are feeling like you are not able to do as well in your school or work because you are having trouble concentrating or calming down, there is nothing wrong with seeking help. You deserve to excel in all that you want to accomplish and you do not have to let ADHD stop you from that.

Do you identify with any of the symptoms that were described for ADHD? If so, which ones?

_____

_____

If you did identify with any of the symptoms, are any of them upsetting to you?

_____

_____

If you feel upset by any of these potential symptoms, who is a safe person that you can talk about it with?

_____

Other Conditions That May Be a Focus

Not everyone is living with a diagnosis. Not to mention, diagnoses may come and go at various points in our lives. Sometimes, people may be going through a hardship but it doesn't mean that they are experiencing a disorder. Some of these might include the following:

- Problems related to family upbringing (parents and/or siblings)
- Divorce, separation, or high conflict within a relationship
- Bereavement (sadness over someone's death)
- Abuse: physical, sexual, emotional, neglect
- Academic or work related problems
- Homelessness or inadequate housing
- Lack of adequate food, poverty, low income
- Phase of life problem: starting or graduating school, leaving home, getting married, starting a new career, becoming a parent, etc.
- Acculturation difficulty, immigration, adjusting to a new culture
- Social exclusion, rejection, bullying, discrimination
- Problems related to health

Do you identify with any of these? Which ones?

_____

_____

_____

How have you handled these stressors?

_____

_____

_____

_____

As you can see, these are just a few of the things that can cause a person to feel unrest. No one's life is perfect and learning to acknowledge what we are struggling with is the first step towards wellbeing. We have to own it. We need to name it. If we are not able to do this, we do not know what we do not know. We are doing the ultimate disservice to ourselves if we do not take the time to learn about these conditions. While it may have been hard to read this chapter (or perhaps you found it incredibly fascinating), I hope that you feel empowered now that you know more.

There are so many other conditions that I could describe and if you find yourself feeling curious, I invite you to learn more. The DSM-5 is the official manual for diagnosis but there are many other books and websites that can provide you with specific information. Again, the disorders that I included are not meant to diagnosis you or help you diagnose someone you know. Rather, they are intended to help you understand a little bit more about what these words mean. We often hear these terms used in passing and I think it is only fair that you have a accurate knowledge for yourself.

Unfortunately, people often place judgment when they are speaking about these conditions, and my hope is that you will be a champion for change in this arena. I hope that you know that people living with these disorders can excel and overcome—perhaps you know this in your own personal life or you have seen a friend or family member attest to this. The next time you hear someone make a derogatory comment or make fun of someone because of his or her disorder, I hope that you will speak up because you now know otherwise. It is essential that we start standing up to the shame that has been attached to mental health. People need to know that we are more than diagnoses and we are not defined by disorders. They may be a piece of us but they are only one part of our complete identity.

Facing It: How to Deal

Now that you've learned about some of the more commonly experienced conditions, what can you actually do about it? Get help! No one should have to succumb to suffering and I'm happy to report that there are SO many ways that people can get help. Whether it's for you or someone you know, you never need to feel like you are alone when it comes to reaching out. In this chapter we'll talk about a variety of things that you can do to help you or someone you know feel better.

Before I dive in, I want to acknowledge how hard it can be though to ask for help. There is a wealth of reasons for why we hold ourselves back.

What do you think are some reasons why people avoid asking for help?

1. _____

2. _____

3. _____

Other reasons might include:

- You worry that people won't believe you or they will think that you're over exaggerating.
- You won't have any friends anymore and/or your significant other will break up with you.
- No one will understand and they will make fun of you behind your back.
- You think you should be able to handle this on your own.

- You think it's just a little thing that eventually will go away on it's own.
- Other people have it way worse than you so you shouldn't complain.
- You deserve to suffer.

The sad truth is that these are just a few of the reasons why people keep the secret of their pain to themselves. They try to hold it in but inevitably, the pain becomes too great and they try to find ways to cope. Unfortunately, these coping methods aren't usually the healthiest or most adaptive. I call these band-aids because they temporarily mask the problem but they do not heal the deep wound that is sitting underneath. What are some of these band-aids?

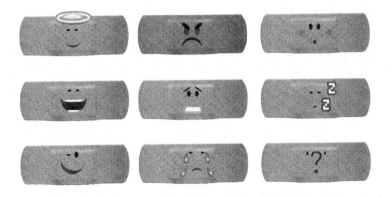

Image credit to Kyle LaFerriere

1. **The perfect angel:** they throw themselves into school and extracurricular activities so they don't have to think or worry about how they actually feel inside.
2. **The angry bird:** they burst out in fits of rage at their parents or even their friends because they hold their feelings inside for so long. Eventually they burst open, seeing nothing but red. They may or may not feel sorry afterward, but they don't spend much time thinking about why they felt upset in the first place.

3. **The bashful passerby:** they avoid making friends and keep to themselves because they don't want to let people in. Or they may have been bullied and are afraid that no one will accept them in the future. They may sit at home playing video games until 4 AM—anything to avoid actual people or real conversations.

4. **The class clown:** always making jokes and never taking much seriously, their lightness keeps them so buoyant that they never have to feel any of their actual pain that is sitting just below the surface.

5. **The anxious student:** they are so worried and stressed out all the time that they are rarely able to laugh and have fun. They constantly feel deprived but they are unable to let go of the control.

6. **The sleeper/eater:** they numb themselves with sleep or food, keeping themselves in a comatose state. You're likely to find them on a Netflix binge where they are much more invested in the storyline of someone else's life rather than their own.

7. **The flirt:** they throw themselves into relationships or anonymous encounters to keep themselves flitting from one fling to the next. By bouncing around, they never have to settle into a relationship and consider what their actual needs and wants might be.

8. **The drama queen:** this person is always having a meltdown of some kind or they are stirring up trouble. Think of your Regina George and her Burn Book. They are so busy spreading rumors and gossip that they never have to look inward at their own struggles.

9. *What's your band-aid that you identify with? How come?*

_____

_____

If we want to truly recover, we have to do some work within and this takes time. The tricky thing about band-aids is that they are so easy to stick on but peeling them off always hurts in the end. So the next time you feel tempted to throw on that band-aid, I invite you to think instead about how else you can cope with your problem. So let's break down some things that you can do to find sustainable relief.

Talk to Family or a Friend

This can feel like the scariest thing to do sometimes. Some of us are lucky and have loved ones that we can turn to no matter what. Others of us do not always have a supportive family and it can leave us feeling that much more isolated. And then there is the really tough situation when our stress and heartache is actually *caused* by our family or loved ones. There is no denying that this can be incredibly painful but I invite you to reach out to someone that you can trust if you need help.

This does not have to be a family or friend necessarily but it should be someone who feels like family to you. Who is that person in your life that you can lean on no matter what? This should be a person that you know wouldn't judge you, doubt you, or belittle you. It's the person who has your back and has an ear for you. I know there is a person out there that values what you have to say and has the time to listen to what you're feeling. You can rely on that person to be a cornerstone for you as you start this journey towards wellbeing.

Even if you feel hesitant to talk to someone—whether it's your family, a friend, or otherwise, I bet you might be surprised by their reaction. More times than not, our loved ones want to support us and I bet it would mean a lot to them if you shared how you felt. Not to mention, when our family knows us well, they can tell when something is up. If they come to you and ask how you're doing, answer honestly. You don't have to say that you're okay when you're not. As hard as it can be to get the conversation started, just own how you feel. Your loved ones will respect your maturity and the fact that you can acknowledge how you truly feel. A great sign of emotional intelligence is someone who can be in touch with all of their feelings on the emotional pie (remember that from the introduction?) rather than a select few.

You'll notice that I asked about family or friends that you could turn to throughout the Name It chapter. That is because different people feel safer to talk to for different situations. It's great to have a few people that you can reach out to; that way you always have a safe haven no matter where you are, who you are with, or what you are doing.

Who are some safe people that you can turn to? What is their relationship in your life?

1. _____

2. _____

3. _____

4. _____

5. _____

Consider the Cultural Context

One thing that I have loved while training to become a psychologist is the emphasis on cultural competence. For the longest time psychology and therapy were tailored for the upper-middle class, Caucasian male. And while this is a part of the population, there were so many ethnicities and cultures that were being ignored. An effective therapist caters to every client and his or her needs, rather than requesting that the client fit themselves into a Westernized mold.

Every culture is different and these differences need to be respected and appreciated. Within this, every culture has a different take on mental health and the aforementioned disorders. Some cultures are very open to talking about mental health while others are not. That is okay. And no matter what culture you come from, you get to decide how you feel about your journey towards mental health. Whether that is with therapy, medication, and/or homeopathic remedies or otherwise, that is your choice.

No matter how you or your culture feels about mental health, it's important to be cognizant of how your family perceives mental illness. Some families and cultures are very open when it comes to mental disorders and want to make sure that their loved ones get the help they need. On the other hand, other cultures and families may see mental health issues as dishonorable or unimportant. But just because your family may view a mental disorder as a stain on the family or not a "real" problem, it does not mean that you should not get help. It's just not worth it. You deserve to get the resources that you need and your family shouldn't prevent you from this. This doesn't mean you have to keep secrets from your family but you should be smart about who you trust with your mental health information. You do not want any potential diagnosis to be held against you—that's not fair. So while I hope your family will have your back, be wise about whom to trust. Make sure you are seeking support from people who will not make you feel guilty for what you are going through.

How would you describe your family's culture?

_____

_____

_____

How do you feel about your culture?

_____

_____

How does your family and culture view mental health?

_____

_____

Does it feel safe to confide in your family about mental health? Why or why not?

_____

_____

This same challenge applies to gender as well. Let's be honest—it's a lot more acceptable for girls and women to talk about their feelings than it is for boys and men. I find this absolutely heartbreaking because guys have feelings and emotions just as much as anyone else. Yet, many of them are forced to keep quiet or they feel too embarrassed, so they apply those band-aids that are ultimately all the more destructive. In fact, while more girls attempt suicide, 78% of all completed suicides are done by males.[31]

If I can stand on my soapbox for a minute, we need to start accepting young men and all the feelings that they have. We cannot judge them when they cry, we cannot get nervous when they say they feel overwhelmed, and we have to help them find ways to process their anger. These are just a few potential feelings that I described; my point is that we need to embrace men and all the emotions they may experience. If we want to live in a culture that equates men and women, then I think we need to make it just as okay for men to express themselves as it is for women.

I also think that women need to be allowed to feel and express their emotions openly as well. While we are given a little more bandwidth for "tolerable" emotions, we are often perceived as emotional, volatile, and even juvenile if we don't always have our "act together." Well, I'm calling this one. I think it's actually a strong and brave woman who is willing to lead and shed a tear at the same time, who says she is offended when someone speaks down to her rather than simply bow her head in deference, and raises her hand once more even though people thinks she has too many ideas. To me, this is an emotionally centered woman and certainly she is a woman that I aspire to be.

Do you think men and women are allowed to express their emotions equally? Why or why not?

_____

_____

What do you think we can do to make all genders feel safer in expressing their emotions?

_____

_____

We have a long way to go when it comes to accepting one another and all of the emotions that we feel. I believe that we feel threatened by emotions because they show a deep and raw vulnerability that is entirely unpredictable. In a world that seeks control and safety (and understandably so), finding and living in these moments of emotional volatility feels like unknown territory. What we don't realize is that when we engage our full emotional spectrum, we are creating profound connections with each other that blow the small talk and social media out of the water. The problem is that we are losing our gumption to encounter these moments. Maybe it's because we are afraid of the potential confrontation, tears, and uncertainty that could ensue. I know that I myself seek solace in my phone or laptop, even when vulnerability is sitting right across from me. But will you join me as I try to lean into these moments of emotionality rather than shy away from them? I think we owe it to the women, men, and our cultural milieu as a whole. We need to embrace one another. Rather than conform to what we believe is expected of us, let's start living as whole-hearted emotional beings, trusting that others will love us that much more for it.

Therapy: What are my Options?

One way to process our emotional experiences is through therapy. A lot of people are skeptical about therapy—I know I was. We often think that going to therapy means you have a problem that you can't deal with alone, that you're going "crazy," or that you're not strong enough. I found all of these assumptions to be proven completely false. While therapy is a place for you to go if you are having a conflict in your life, it can also be a place to help you works towards self-improvement. Plenty of healthy and high-functioning people go to therapy—it's not just for those struggling with a disorder or a crisis.

I found this to be true in my own personal experience. I have been to therapy a few times in my life. I first went to therapy when I was a teenager to work on better communication with my mom. I didn't necessarily want to go but my mom recommended it for us. We went to sessions together and I remember being nervous at first. But by the end of the first session, I felt so comfortable with the therapist that I was able to talk openly about my feelings with both she and my mom present. Our relationship improved and we both agreed that it was a good choice for us.

I also went to therapy recently for premarital counseling. It was so nice for my partner and I to have space to concretely discuss all that marriage includes—finances, family choices, and religion, just to name a few. I ended up enjoying the experience so much that I did some of my own personal therapy with our psychologist afterward. While it really challenged me and made me look inward, I'm so thankful for the insight that it provided. I know that I grew during that experience and the feedback my therapist provided was immeasurably valuable.

Therapy is not necessarily easy. We often go to therapy in hopes that we will immediately feel better. We secretly wish that our therapist will be like a magic genie that can grant our wishes or tell us what we have to do. But that's not a good therapist. A good therapist will not give advice; instead a great therapist will walk alongside you in your journey to empower you to make your own decisions. Our hope as therapists is that we can increase your self-esteem, build up your confidence, and help you advocate for yourself.

So what does therapy exactly include? Every therapist is a little different and you may want to meet with a few before you decide who is the best fit for you. Typically therapy is about 50 minutes per week where you sit in a room with your therapist and talk about whatever you'd like to talk about. While initially your therapist will probably have a lot of questions about your life history (we call this an intake), eventually the sessions will shift where you will decide what you want to focus on. Some clients like to come prepared to session knowing what they want to talk about that week. Other clients aren't sure and they wait to see what comes up. Either way is perfectly okay.

The length of therapy is different for each person. Some people are in therapy for only a few sessions and other people go to therapy for years. It all depends on what you're going through and if you're enjoying the process. What I would recommend is attending at least five sessions of therapy with a therapist you like before you really decide whether or not it is working for you. So much of therapy is about the fit; in other words, do you and your therapist get along? What's most important is that you feel safe and cared for by your therapist. So long as you feel like your therapist values you, the research shows that you are much more likely to have a successful therapeutic experience.[32]

While therapy is sometimes an individual experience, with just you and the therapist, there are many different variations of therapy. As a therapist in training, I have worked with couples, siblings, parents and children, and roommates. So much of our wellbeing is based on our relationships so it makes sense that we provide therapy from a systemic standpoint. So if you having conflict in your life, either with a parent, a friend, or dating partner, therapy can be a great place to process the conflict and come up with some more effective communicative strategies.

Group therapy is also an option. I have seen so many clients love this experience because they appreciate seeing that they are not alone in their pain. There is a group out there for everyone. Perhaps you have a family member who is an alcoholic, Al-Anon provides amazing groups to support you. Or you have a family member who is struggling with mental illness. The National Alliance on Mental Illness (NAMI) has incredible support groups so that you can hear from others who are going through the same thing. There are also groups for eating disorders, grief, school stress—just about anything you can imagine. You never have to feel like you are alone and there are plenty of people who have your back.

Maybe this is piquing your interest but you still have doubts. Is therapy confidential? Can I trust my therapist no matter what? Let me clarify. While therapy is an absolutely confidential space, there are a few caveats. Your therapist wants to respect you and your privacy but there are a few instances where therapists are mandated reporters. This means that your therapist has to notify an outside source, like the police or the Department of Children and Family Services for example, if they believe that you are in danger. While your therapist should tell you this in the first session, I will tell you here so that you are fully informed. What are the five instances?

1. **Child abuse:** If you are under the age of 18 or you tell the therapist about someone who is under the age of 18 who is being abused, the therapist will need to break confidentiality to get the child the help that they need. This abuse includes physical abuse (hitting, slapping, kicking, etc.), sexual abuse, and emotional abuse (name-calling, yelling, threatening). It also includes neglect (preventing the child from adequate food, shelter, and water, etc.). Reporting also takes place if the person that committed the abuse still has access to children.

2. **Elder abuse:** If someone older than the age of 65 is being abused in any way (financial abuse, physical abuse, sexual abuse, emotional abuse, and neglect), the therapist will need to let the Adult Protective Services know.

3. **Dependent adult abuse:** If someone who is between the ages of 18 and 64 is being abused and they are either physically handicapped or intellectually impaired, the therapist will need to let the Adult Protective Services know.

4. **Suicide or self-harm:** If you tell the therapist that you are planning to hurt yourself, whether this includes cutting, burning, attempting suicide, etc., the therapist will very likely need to seek outside help to protect you.

5. **Hurting others:** If you tell the therapist that you intend to harm someone or you know of someone who could be in grave danger, the therapist may take action to protect the potential victims.

I know that's a mouthful but I think it's important that you have full transparency when it comes to therapy. You deserve to know what therapy entails, and while your therapist wants to protect your confidentiality as much as possible, they also want to make sure that they help keep you and others safe.

If you're reading this and you are under 18, you may be wondering about how therapy works when parents are involved. Every therapist is a little different in this regard and you should ask your therapist if you want to know more. Some therapists talk very openly with the parents of their child client, letting them know what you talked about in every session. Other therapists are very quiet about what their clients talk about, only telling the parents what they absolutely have to know (the child is in danger, the child is having thoughts of harming themselves, etc.). There are also instances where therapists are willing to work with you without your parents' knowledge. This varies state by state and depends on how old you are (typically at least 14 years of age), but if you have something that you want to talk about with complete confidentiality without your parents finding out, there may be a therapist who is willing to help you out. Just remember that you never have to be alone and there is someone that is more than willing to sit with you and listen to your story.

Have you ever been in therapy before? If so, what was your experience like?

_____

_____

Do you have any hesitation about going to therapy?

_____

_____

What would you want to talk about in therapy?

_____

_____

_____

_____

Exercise

Believe it or not, exercise is one of the biggest recommendations for clients, especially those that are struggling with depression. One study showed that while medication can have equally successful results upon the completion of treatment, exercise helps with long-lasting benefits that are sustainable months after treatment.[33] Now I know exercising may seem that much more difficult when you're down in the dumps, but the positive effects are so worth it. When you take the time to move (if only for a little while each day), your brain releases feel-good chemicals like endorphins, positive neurotransmitters (think dopamine, serotonin, etc.), and it may reduce immune system chemicals that increase depression. Exercise is also great for helping you feel more confident in your body, distracting you from anxiety, and it may even provide opportunities to socialize with others (dance class, basketball team, swim meets, etc.).[34]

It really doesn't take much, either. One my favorite studies looked at 20 students' brains while they were taking a test. Half of the students sat quietly before the test and half of the students took a 20 minute walk beforehand. There is a noticeable difference when you look at the MRI images of the brains. The students who took walks had brains had brains that were much more activated during the test.[35]

Our brains are incredibly amazing and taking the time to add some fitness to our routine is a wonderful, natural remedy to treat any sadness or stress you may feel. Now I know some of us like exercise more than others (to be honest with you, I don't love it), but I think we can all agree that it is good for us. What are some ideas for helping you add more exercise to your schedule?

1. **Switch it up:** No one likes monotony. Add variety to your exercise regimen by swimming on Mondays, hiking on Wednesdays, and biking on Fridays.
2. **Some is better than none:** Many of us think we either have to go hard core with our exercise or do nothing at all. Remember, just a little bit can go a long way. Walk around the block, clean your room, play hide and seek with the kid you babysit. These little things make a difference.
3. **Put your shoes on:** The hardest part is starting. Just put your sneakers on and go. It also helps to add your exercise routine to your calendar or schedule so you feel more obligated to actually show up.

What kind of exercise do you like to do?

_____

_____

What holds you back from exercising?

_____

_____

What can you commit to this month to help you improve your fitness routine?

Medication

Another option for some people is the use of medication. Now obviously this is not a pharmacology textbook where I'm going to tell you about every medication that's on the market, but I think it is very necessary that you learn more if medication may be part of the picture for you or a loved one. Always find out about the dosage, the symptoms that the medication is supposed to treat, and the side effects. And while it is not my job to convince you of whether or not you should look into medication, I will say that the best thing you can do is to keep an open mind.

I know that I was very much against medication before I started my Master's program in Marriage and Family Therapy. If you asked me why I was so anti-meds, I'm not sure that I would have had a good answer. I was always given an underlying message that medication was not "good" for you and it meant you were weak. Tough it out, I thought.

Back up. I now know how helpful medication can be with certain illnesses and for certain people. I have seen medication be a life-saver for some of my clients and I now see how I foolish I was to hold a blanket statement that all medication is bad. However, I also know that there has been a 68% increase in prescriptions for girls and a 30% increase for boys in the past decade.[36] Sometimes the path of least resistance is handing out medication instead of doing the deep work of therapy or teaching other coping skills.

Ultimately medication is a very nuanced decision. It is a highly personal choice and while it is sometimes very necessary (like for schizophrenia and bipolar disorder), other times it is more of a conversation between you and a psychiatrist. What is most important is that you do not judge others or de-value yourself if medication is on the table. Just because someone takes medication it doesn't make him or her any less of a person. They are not weak; rather they are strong for seeking the most appropriate help for themselves. It is so easy for us to judge others, but we must remember that we are not only not walking in their shoes, we are not living in their brain either.

Do you have any questions about medication? Who can you ask to help you understand?

Spirituality and Faith

Implementing spirituality, faith, and/or religion is such a personal choice. For some people, their beliefs can provide them with a tremendous sense of healing. You have to seek resources that will be the most helpful to you. I respect all people of all faiths and non-faiths and as someone who has counseled people who are Protestant, Jewish, Catholic, Muslim, Buddhist, and Atheist, I see how spirituality is such a unique experience for every person.

I wanted to specifically include spirituality in this book because there are so many people who rely on their faith, especially when there is a challenge. We know that when someone is suffering, religion is one of the first places people turn to for help.[37] For example, in a study looking at people diagnosed with a serious mental illness in Los Angeles, 80% of them turned to their religion to help them cope and 65% of them indicated that their faith helped them reduce their symptoms.[38] Faith may also play a preventative role: those who are spiritual have lower levels of depression (especially when experiencing severe life stressors).[39]

I will say that in my own life, my faith has provided me a great deal of hope in my darkest times. Finding a quiet time to pray and reflect on my relationship with God is something that I value. I also enjoy the healing experience of praying with other people and feeling a communal sense of caring. I have loved having a church community filled with many people that I can trust. I'll be honest in saying that my walk with faith has ebbed and flowed throughout the years but it's a journey that I am glad to grow in nonetheless. I give thanks for my faith and I hope that it will continue to develop as I age.

So, whether or not you are spiritual and/or religious, perhaps this is a good time to reflect on this experience in your life. I am not trying to sway you one way or the other; all that I am asking is for you to consider if this could be a helpful component to your life. Maybe it's worth visiting some churches, synagogues, and/or temples and deciding for yourself if it could be helpful for you. I always believe that the more information we have, the better decision we can make. Spirituality looks different for everyone but I would invite you to consider if it could be valuable for you.

What is your experience with religion and/or spirituality?

_____

_____

_____

Do you think it could be helpful in your life? Why or why not?

_____

_____

_____

No One Way

These were just a few ideas for what you can do to cope in effective ways. Every person is different and what works well for some might not work as well for others. It takes time to work towards true healing and we have to be patient with ourselves as we try to remedy ourselves from within. While it is so easy to throw on those band-aids to get through the day, I challenge you to the deep work that is necessary for longstanding growth and change. It may be more painful in the short term as you take a close look at what you need to change in your life, but ultimately, you are doing yourself the greatest service by looking inward. Please know that people are here for you as you work through that journey.

What About When It's More Serious?

One of the biggest frustrations that I hear among young adults is that they feel like their problems are being ignored. So much gets swept under the rug because people don't want to "deal with it." One story I heard has stuck with me, and I think it's all too accurate. There was a group of high school girls that volunteered together and while they were friendly with each other, they only saw each other when at charity events. You can imagine their shock and dismay when they found out that one of the girls in their group had completed suicide. The girls were grief stricken by the news and they wanted to talk about it with one another. They were even more upset when they met with their mothers the next week—not to talk about what happened to the member, but to meet for a formal social gathering. The girl's name was not mentioned once.

This story happens every day. We have classmates, co-workers, and friends who take their life, and rather than processing our grief, their name and story gets whispered away. The only way we get to come to terms with what happened is through text messages and murmurings, rather than a space to openly talk about what happened and how we can prevent it in the future.

Talking about suicide is something I'm passionate about. I know people shy away from the subject because it makes them feel uncomfortable, but honestly, we have to talk about it. We are losing too many people to suicide and I will not stand by silently. If we are going to help one another, we need to start talking publicly about how we can prevent this. Will you join me in this effort?

A few notes before we talk about the subject of suicide. First, I know how triggering suicide can be. Talking about it may bring back memories for you that are extremely painful and I want to be mindful of that. Please know that I completely respect you and your feelings and if this feels too overwhelming, please read this chapter another time. I think this is pertinent information that everyone should learn about at some point but do not push yourself if you are feeling too uncomfortable.

There are a lot of reasons I care so much about this topic. Maybe it's the fact that "suicide contagion" is a real thing. When someone takes their life, those who knew the person (whether it was a classmate or colleague) are at a higher risk of attempting or completing suicide themselves.[40] Or it's the fact that in the past 50 years, suicide rates for those between the ages of 15-24 have increased by over 200%. When we break down the numbers, we know that 12 students in this age group are taking their lives every single day. That's one person every two hours.[41] So in the time it takes to go to lacrosse practice, take an exam, or go out to dinner, a young adult will have taken their life. Knowing this, you bet I am going to talk about this issue.

We need to do something about this. And quickly. The emotional health of college freshmen has declined to its lowest point in 25 years with only 52% currently reporting that their emotional health is above average. In fact, 6% of undergraduate students have seriously thought about taking their life. What's even scarier? Nearly half of them didn't tell anyone.

What are some reasons that students are holding back from sharing with others? They may be afraid of judgment or they think they are beyond help. They worry that they will look "insane" or that no one will understand. But here's one of the biggest myths about suicide: we think that talking about it inclines someone to complete the act. It's the opposite. Talking openly with someone about their thoughts and feelings surrounding suicide helps them process their pain and may actually help prevent action from being taken.[42]

Much of the time someone attempts to take their life, it is *not* because they want to die. They want to stop the pain. Sometimes the grief can feel so agonizing that it feels unbearable to survive it. Yet if people can work through their temporary feelings of extreme suffering, they are much more likely to overcome their grief and find a reason to live once more. This is especially important when a teenager is thinking about suicide. Because the frontal lobe of the brain is not fully developed until age 25 (this is the part of the brain that has long term planning ability and understands consequences), a teen brain can make sudden decisions that have permanent effects. Because the teen brain does not fully understand outcomes, the notion of suicide as a long-lasting decision is not always processed. So a sudden idea or impulse, like the thought of attempting suicide, can quickly become a forever fate. This is doubly complicated by the fact that the teen brain often has a higher reactive response to emotional experiences more than a child or adult brain would have.[43] For example, love is that much sweeter and anger is that much more bitter for an adolescent than at any other age in life. Naturally then, when a teenager feels painful or upsetting experiences, it can feel especially devastating.

Parts of the Human Brain

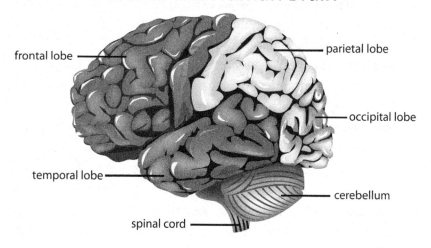

What are some of these stressful experiences that are triggering some students?

- **Pressure to perform academically:** Get the best grades, get into the top university, and land the best honors. Everyone is so competitive and you feel like you can't keep up. Why even try?

- **Family drama:** Parents are having difficulty in their relationship or you can't get along with your sibling. You feel like the black sheep of your family or you feel like you are a disappointment to them.

- **Bullying:** You are excluded on Snapchat or your ex-group of friends intentionally doesn't invite you to the upcoming party. You get beat up or they call you names when you walk down the hallway.

- **You lived through something traumatic:** The world doesn't feel the same anymore. You thought you could trust others and that idea seems shattered now. You can't relax anymore.

- **Financial stress:** You have no money to accomplish your goals. You can't afford a car, you have student loans will that will take forever to repay, and you definitely can't afford to take someone on a nice date.

- **You feel insecure:** You've gained some weight while it looks like everyone else around you is blossoming. You hate your hair, you have acne, or people make fun of your clothes.

- **You broke up:** You thought they were the love of your life and then they cheated on you. Or they're just not into the relationship anymore. You've never felt so unwanted in your life.

- **You fell short:** You didn't make the varsity soccer team and all your other friends did. You tried out for the school play and didn't even make the chorus. You got denied admission to your dream school.

- **You feel depressed:** Or anxious. You've been feeling low for such a long time, you're not sure if it will ever end. You just want the suffering to stop.

Can you identify with any of these? Are there any other reasons why you may feel upset?

_____

_____

When we look at this list, it makes sense why young adults are feeling so incredibly overwhelmed. We need to pay attention to these signs. We need to listen and look out for each other if we see one another struggling. I believe that students are under an inordinate amount of stress and we need to watch out for them. What are some of the signs to look out for when it comes to suicide risk?

- The person talks about suicide, death, or having no reason to live. They seem preoccupied with death or the idea of dying.
- They are having trouble sleeping or eating. They have gained or lost a lot of weight recently and they are sleeping more or less than usual.
- Their behavior has suddenly changed. They are more energetic or are they moving much slower than their normal pace.
- They have pulled back from friends, family, and the activities that they used to love. They don't seem interested in school, work, or their hobbies.
- They are giving away their beloved possessions—this could include clothes, instruments, even pets.
- They don't seem to care about their appearance anymore. They are not showering, dressing nicely, or grooming themselves.

- They have a prior history of suicidal behavior, either personally or they have a family history or friends who have attempted or completed suicide.
- They are struggling with a mental disorder like depression, anxiety, bipolar disorder, schizophrenia or another diagnosis.
- They are struggling with substance abuse.
- They have become more aggressive, impulsive, or agitated.
- They have access to firearms or other objects that could be used to hurt themselves.

Now that you know these signs, you need to be prepared to do something about it if you or someone you know is in danger. If someone comes to you and says they are thinking about suicide, if you see the signs in someone else, or if you are experiencing any of these signs, it's important to talk about it. We often feel so afraid to have these conversations because we are worried people will judge us, that no one will take it seriously, or we're scared we will make someone angry. While these potential outcomes can be uncomfortable, it is always worth saving a life. So how can you navigate these conversations?

1. **Talk openly about suicide:** Unfortunately, suicide has become such a "Voldemort" word that we've become too nervous to talk honestly about it. But the best thing you can do is have a real conversation with someone if they are thinking about suicide. You can ask the following:
   - Have you thought about attempting suicide?
   - Do you have a plan?
   - What is your timeline for making an attempt?
   - Do you have access to any objects that you could use to hurt yourself?

2. **Based on their answers, get immediate help:** Don't wait. Seek urgent help if the person says they plan on hurting themselves in the near future. Especially if they have a plan, have access to an object that they could use to hurt themselves, and they have a timeline, take immediate action. This includes:

   - Telling either your parent(s), their parent(s), and/or a teacher.
   - Calling 911.
   - Calling a suicide hotline number.
   - Don't leave the person alone until you have brought another person to help you.
   - Remove any lethal means of self-harm: Take away any pills, sharp objects, or firearms that the person may have access to.
   - Encourage them to seek professional help with a therapist.
   - Protect yourself: If the person is physically dangerous or is threatening you in any way, your safety comes first. You should protect yourself first before taking further action.

3. **Don't worry about this person getting mad at you:** You may be worried that the suicidal person will get angry with you if you seek outside help. They may have said, "You promised you wouldn't tell" or "I thought I could trust you." Here is what you can say back:

   - I value you so incredibly much. I had to get help for you because I love you and care about you and I want to have you in my life for years to come.
   - I know you're angry with me but I want to look out for you. You mean so much to many people and we need you around.

- Even though you're upset with me, I still want to be friends with you and I am always here for you. I am doing my very best to help you and I hope you would do the same for me if the roles were reversed.

4. **Be there for the person:** If someone confides in you that that they feel suicidal, remember that it takes a lot of guts to reach out to someone. The best thing that you can do is listen patiently. Don't judge the person or blame them for feeling the way they do. True empathy is siting with someone in their grief and giving them space to process how they feel. As shocked, hurt, or scared as you may be (which is perfectly understandable), don't make it about you.

5. **Get professional help:** Remember, while you can be there for someone when they are feeling suicidal, it is not your job to provide 24/7 care for someone. If someone is suicidal, they should be under the care of a professional therapist who is trained to handle suicide. It is not your responsibility to save someone's life and the best thing you can do is help guide them to people who are prepared for these situations. You may also want to seek your own therapeutic care as it can be incredibly stressful to help someone who is suicidal.

Let me check in with you. I know this is a lot of information to process. You may be feeling triggered reading or learning about suicide. You may be reminded of someone you know who attempted suicide or completed it. That person may have been a best friend, a family member, or even yourself. Take a minute to catch your breath. Treat yourself kindly and gently.

You might be having memories come up. When this happens, I will often hear people say, "I should have done this..." or "I could have done that, and maybe it would have saved my loved one's life." "If only." Hindsight is 20/20 as they say. We can never predict what other people will do. If you have lost someone to suicide or there has been a close call, don't blame yourself for a second. We are all doing the best we can with the information we have. We can never punish ourselves for the "should have" and "could have" moments in our lives. There is no way we can know what will happen. The best thing we can do is equip ourselves with knowledge and start having these conversations more openly. I want to commend you on reading this chapter, as hard as it may have been. I know it's not easy to talk about suicide but the more we learn to deal with this in an open manner, the more lives we can hopefully save.

What feelings are coming up for you as you are learning about suicide?

_____

_____

_____

What steps will you take if you or someone you know is suicidal? (Hint: the steps are listed in the chapter).

1. _____

2. _____

3. _____

4. _____

5. _____

6. _____

Embracing It: How to Talk About Mental Health

One of the best ways to begin integrating mental health in our lives is to begin talking about it openly with others. While we can learn about it (naming it) and empower ourselves by seeking out resources (facing it), we also have to begin looking out for each other (embracing it). This is a two-fold experience. We need to be open to hearing from others and we need to begin reaching out to those that we see in need.

Now there are a few different situations I'm going to cover. We'll talk first about how to handle conversations when they are directed towards you. We'll also cover how to have conversations with family members, friends, significant others, and acquaintances. We'll also talk about the Stages of Change so that you have a better understanding of how people work through their challenges.

I know these conversations aren't always easy or fun, but they are crucial. If you want to have open and honest relationships with the people you love, it means that you have to talk about these things at some point. Avoiding, denying, or minimizing the problem only makes the situation worse. When you can talk about mental health in a safe way, your relationships will be that much stronger.

I Need to Talk to Someone

You may be reading this and having that tickle in your stomach that you need help. We talked in an earlier chapter about reaching out to family and friends and that's usually the best place to turn to for guidance. Getting help and starting the conversation is the hardest part. It feels risky. You might worry that your family and friends will judge you, they won't understand, or they will think you're overreacting. If they have any of those responses or criticisms, then it's best to reach out to a professional. They work with mental health challenges on a daily basis and are well-equipped to help you.

But how do you begin this conversation? Even telling a professional (who is a stranger) about your hardship can feel just as tough as telling a family member. How can you get through this conversation?

1. **Think about what you want to say.** Maybe it will help you to write it down, to say it in front of the mirror, or to listen to some music that expresses how you are feeling.
2. **Reach out to the person who you truly trust and ask to talk to them in a quiet and private space.** Or if this feels too intense, try talking to the person when you're walking together or driving in the car together. Sometimes less eye contact can make it easier for you to get the words out.
3. **Once you've said your piece, give the person a moment to react.** They may be surprised, upset, or concerned. Especially if they didn't see this coming, they may need some time to process.
4. **Provide education for them:** We all carry around myths and stigmas about mental health. Just as you are learning about mental health, provide the person with resources so that they can learn more themselves.
5. **Find normality together:** Make time to do something you enjoy together so that the relationship doesn't feel centered solely around mental health. It might feel a little awkward after you've talked with the person but you should be intentional about getting back to activities you enjoy together so that you can feel comfortable once more.

Ultimately, that person you confide in should be there to support you. They shouldn't make the conversation about them. Instead, the discussion should be about you, your feelings, and the next best steps to take if you need help. Again, if the person doesn't have that response, I highly recommend seeking a professional who is concerned solely about your wellbeing.

Someone Wants to Talk to Me

What do you do when someone comes up to you and says, "Hey, do you have a minute to talk? I wanted to talk about something with you." Your stomach probably drops in that moment. No one likes hearing this and we all feel nervous in that moment. Your mind races. What could they possibly have to say? Are they going to embarrass me? Are they going to accuse me? Am I going to cry? Your mind may be brewing with all kinds of ideas and you may be filled with a sense of dread. But as painful as it is in that moment, hit the pause button. Take a deep breath. Give the person a chance and hear them out.

They may say any number of things. Maybe they have noticed that you've lost a lot of weight recently (or gained some weight). They are saying that you seem depressed or they have seen you really anxious lately. They might say that they saw scratches on your arms or they think you're drinking too much. "I'm worried about you," they say. Woah. That can feel like a lot to hear.

Maybe your secret is out. Or you may be in denial and what they are saying can't possibly be true. Or, maybe they are generally off in their concern—that's okay—it happens sometimes. It's better to have a false alarm than a missed warning. What really matters is that you hear this message: "I am concerned because *I care about you.*" If this is a person who loves you, they will inevitably say this in their message to you. They know that it's not easy to hear the words they are telling you. And it's just as hard for them to say the words to you as it is to hear them. It takes a lot of courage to reach out to someone who you are worried about—you never know how someone will receive the message.

There are many ways that you can react to someone after they've said that they are concerned about you. You can lash out—you can accuse them, get angry with them, and even walk out on them. You can ignore them and say that there is nothing to be concerned about. You can push them away and get back at them. Sure, these are all things you can do. And frankly, it's probably easier in the moment to have one of these responses than to respond in the most helpful way possible.

As much as it hurts, sometimes, your answer might be: "You're right." You can finally acknowledge that you are struggling with depression, or bulimia, or ADHD—whatever it might be. You can finally own that you are having a hard time and that's okay. There is nothing to be ashamed of. It's not like you are intentionally doing this to yourself to get attention (and anyone who accuses you of that is lacking information about what it means to live with a mental disorder). The minute you can tell someone that you need help is a moment of herculean strength. It shows incredible maturity, grit, and wisdom. No one can fault you for it. If anything, people will admire your honesty.

A great example of this comes from the late Carrie Fisher (known her for role as Princess Leia in *Star Wars*). I love how she completely owned her experience with mental health. She was diagnosed with Bipolar Disorder and never denied it or minimized it a day in her life. She said, "I am mentally ill. I can say that. I am not ashamed of that. I survived that, I'm still surviving it, but bring it on."

So while it's never easy to admit that you need to help to someone, almost always you will be glad that you did. The second you step into your truth, you can begin getting the help that you need.

And if the person is genuinely wrong? If you truly do not have a disorder? That's alright. No one ever knows the full story. Kindly say to them that you really appreciate their concern but you are doing okay. Let them know that if you did have a problem, you would tell them. It's easy to be mad at someone for "assuming" something about you but rather than get defensive, see their decision to reach out as an example of their love for you.

I'm Worried About my Family Member

While you would hope that families would be forthcoming about their challenges, that is not always the case. Families can contain deep vaults of secrets that they don't even tell each other. Everyone has their own reasons for keeping their mental health private, but if the family as a whole is suffering, then it's worth talking about.

I've dealt with this myself. I had a few family members who have struggled with alcoholism and it's caused me incredible distress over the years. But when our family members hurt us in this way, it is because they are hurting just as much, if not more so. It's so unfortunate that they unintentionally or intentionally inflict this pain upon the people who love them the most but it is often because they are so overwhelmed by their experience. They need help and they haven't been able to receive it. They haven't been able to help themselves.

Some of my family members have passed away because of their addictions and other family members are working to overcome their substance use. It's not a perfect picture with a happy ending all the time. The reality is, not everyone is ready to get help. Denial is incredibly powerful and making changes can hurt—even though it's better in the long run. It can feel incredibly selfish when our family members put their substance use, their mania, or their mental disorder above us, but oftentimes, it is because they are such a victim to their experience. Without help, many disorders can become so overwhelming that they can take over our lives, if we are not careful. Unfortunately, family members get caught in this wreckage just because they are close by.

But just because someone in your family is hurting, it doesn't mean that you have to get hurt as well. You are in control of your own life and as you grow up, you can decide what your response will be towards that person. Every family and situation is different but in general, and based on my own experience, here is what I recommend when it comes to talking with a family member who is suffering or struggling with a mental disorder, including substance use.

1. **Have a one-on-one conversation:** Even though there may be a lot of people in your family, it's best to talk about your concern with the person directly. Ideally, you should have the conversation when you are both calm and removed from triggering situations. Crying, screaming, and showing signs of anger will only amplify the problem. You don't want the family member to feel ganged up on or attacked and they are more likely to feel this way if everyone is talking to them at once.

   - An exception to this is planning an intervention. This can be very effective when someone is struggling with substance use. Interventions can be intense but powerful experiences and you should seek a professional to guide you in the process if you think your family member would benefit from this.

2. **Check in with the person:** Especially if you are living with this family member, it's important to continue talking about the challenge on a fairly regular basis. It's easy to fall into the pattern of avoidance (or even enabling where you help the person maintain their behavior) because the conversation may be so uncomfortable. But you owe it to yourself and the family member to check in every now and then to make sure they are okay. You don't want to nag the person and bring up the problem every day—especially if you feel angry or hurt—but you do want to make sure the person knows that you haven't stopped caring about them.

3. **Seek your own support:** Chances are, you are in quite a bit of pain yourself if you are watching a loved one suffer. You should have your own space to process any shock, grief, or disappointment you may feel. There are many support groups that can guide you through your experience (NAMI or Al-Anon, for example). You can also see a therapist if you want to talk privately about your experience.

4. **Let it go:** After you've talked with the person, there is only so much you can do. Remember that you are not your family member's therapist and it is not up to you to save them. People can only help themselves as much as they are willing to accept it. You cannot force someone to get help and expect that they will make long-lasting changes. At some point, you have to trust that you have done your part—you have spoken up— and that is the best you can do. Don't ever blame yourself if a family member is unwilling to make changes in their life. You can play the "If I did this" or "I should have done that" game all day, but ultimately, it is the person's choice whether or not they want to get help.

5. **Break the cycle:** One of the best ways to heal is to create the change you wished your family member would make. Be conscious about the decisions you make in your life. Be proactive. Personally, I know based on my family history with drinking that I need to be careful. Therefore, I hardly ever drink and I have chosen a partner who rarely drinks as well. I don't live in a culture of partying (not only because it reminds me of painful memories) but because I don't want to make myself susceptible to those temptations. And while some disorders are genetic and out of our control, like bipolar disorder and schizophrenia, you can still learn about these conditions and learn about treatment options should you or another family receive one of these diagnoses. Education is power and you do have control over that.

I realize how hard these situations can be. I've lived through it myself and it's provided some of the most painful memories in my life. It's never easy but I'm glad that I haven't ignored my family's problems. I've faced it. I hope that you can as well; not only for your family member's sake, but for your peace of mind as well.

Be kind to yourself as you're learning to have these conversations. It takes practice. I owe so much to my therapist because she helped me learn how to effectively have these kinds of confrontations. Before I worked with my therapist I tried so many other faulty ways. I tried crying, I tried ignoring the person, and I tried making passive aggressive comments. None of it worked—the person kept drinking every time.

What ultimately worked? Talking to the person and making the conversation about them. In the past I always made it about myself. I would say things like, "You're hurting me so much" and "How could you do this to our family?" But this time I made it about them. I said to the person, "You have so much potential and alcohol is getting in the way of that. I have seen you accomplish so many amazing things and you're being held back by your drinking. I know you are so much better than this." The night of that conversation, the person said they would stop drinking. I wasn't sure if I believed them but now, five months later as I write this, they still haven't had a drink.

Now if you've lived with a similar experience, you and I both know that we can't have false faith in this change. As happy as I am about my family member's time of sobriety, I know that I cannot be too self-assured. Mental health challenges can be more like riding waves than climbing a mountain. I wish I could say that it gets better and better but each day we make a new choice about how we will approach a tough situation. I'm so proud of my family member for taking these positive steps, but it is an effort that is required daily.

Be patient with your family members as they do the best that they can. Be proud of the positive changes that they are making. And if they fall (as they might), do what you need to do for your sake. Whether that's standing by them or seeking your own support, you have to do what is best for you and your family. I know these situations are incredibly tricky and downright hard, but I know that you will get through it. Please know that you are never alone in this.

Is there a family member that comes to mind that you believe needs help? If so, what kind of help do you think they need?

_____

_____

How does this family member's struggle impact your life?

_____

_____

What can you do to get the support that you need?

_____

_____

I'm Worried About my Friend or Significant Other

What do you do when you're concerned about a good friend or your partner? You've noticed that they aren't talking with you as much, that they aren't going to school or work as often, or they seem angry. You have seen these changes for weeks now—you can't ignore it. What do you do?

Talk to them. Confrontation is never easy but it's the most compassionate thing that you can do for someone you love. You may be worried about risking the friendship or the relationship but that is less of a cost than risking someone's overall wellbeing. Even if you've only known the person for a short while, it's worth talking to them if you are worried.

What are some signs that you should be talking to the person?

- **Your partner or friend is acting different in any way:** This could be a whole bunch of different signs but if you see any of the symptoms we talked about in the earlier chapters and you notice that your friend or partner seems distressed or avoidant, try to talk with them.
- **You notice that other people are talking about it:** This is one of the biggest clues. If others are picking up on your friend or partner's behavior (and gossiping about it), then the person deserves to know that you are personally concerned. When you approach your friend or partner, don't tell them what others have said, though. This will likely make them feel worse—no one likes to be talked about without their knowledge.
- **It's keeping you up at night:** If you find yourself thinking about this friend or partner and you are worrying about them on a regular basis, it means that it's time to reach out. Trust your gut on this one.

What next? You ask your friend or partner to talk. You're probably feeling so nervous. You imagine every possible scenario and you're so worried that this will ruin your relationship or friendship. What if you offend them? What if you're wrong? Or what if you're right and they're not willing to get help? All these situations can feel so scary. And the reality is, you can't predict how they will react. The only thing you have control over is your words. The best thing you can do is say that you care about the person, offer to help them in any way, and leave it at that. The ball is in their court at that point.

Be prepared for any number of responses. They might be defensive, angry, or hurt. These are all just exterior responses that mask how they are truly feeling inside. Your friend or partner, if truly struggling, is probably experiencing so much pain and letting others in on that pain can feel like a shameful experience. Even though you are approaching them with nothing but love and support, it still feels like a big admission—especially since we have come to believe that we should be "perfect" at all times. Showing others that we are flawed and struggling can make us feel incredibly vulnerable and not everyone is able to do that instantaneously. So what can you do after you've talked to them?

1. **Let them know you're here for them:** Once you've said your piece, you don't need to keep bringing it up on a daily basis. The person knows what you think and trust that they will approach you when they are ready. If a few weeks or months go by and nothing has changed, you probably want to try talking to them again—especially if your gut is telling you that something is wrong.

2. **Don't spread the gossip:** People can be very curious when it comes to mental health. Keep this between you and your friend or partner. If you truly support them, you will respect their privacy.

3. **Know when to walk away:** Sometimes a friend or partner just isn't ready to get the help they need. That is not your fault. If a friend or partner is going down a truly destructive path and isn't willing to get help (or is trying to take you down with them), sometimes the best thing you can do is to end the friendship or relationship. You need to protect your own mental health, and if the person is causing you suffering, you shouldn't be expected to stay in that friendship or relationship forever.

Is there a friend that you're concerned about?

_____

_____

If you have a partner, are you concerned about them in any way?

_____

_____

What can you do to reach out to this friend or partner?

_____

_____

Is there anything that you're worried about when it comes to approaching this friend or partner?

_____

_____

What will you do if the friend or partner isn't willing to get help?

_____

_____

Protecting our Minority Friends

We need to especially look out for our friends and loved ones who are people of color, LGBTQ, not able bodied, intellectually impaired, and/or have any other experience that includes them in minority populations. People in one or more of these groups experience more discrimination, prejudice, bullying, and trauma than others and this can lead them to have more challenges with their mental health, known as "minority stress." In fact, we know that people within the LGBTQ community are almost three times more likely to experience a disorder like depression or anxiety. This can have real effects: LGBTQ youth are four times more likely to attempt suicide and 38-65% of transgender individuals experience what is called suicidal ideation—or thoughts about taking their own life.

Ethnic minorities endure real consequences from this minority stress as well. Just these statistics alone floor me:[44]

- African Americans are 20% more likely to report that they are experiencing serious mental distress than their Caucasian counterparts.
- Suicide attempts for Latina girls between grades 9-12 were 70% higher than Caucasian girls of the same age in 2011.
- Adolescent American Indian/Alaska Native females have death rates pertaining to mental health almost four times the rate of White females in the same age group.

These numbers prove how necessary it is for us to look out for one another. It's so important that we serve as allies for minority communities. Especially if you are a family member or close friend to someone that is a part of one or more of these groups, it's crucial that you express empathy. Even if someone's values are different than your own (which is okay), we still need to embrace each other with acceptance. I am not saying that you have to like everything that a person does, but I believe that we can still compassionately accept each other regardless.

When we are cruel to one another, there are real consequences. For example, when a LGBTQ person comes out that they are gay, lesbian, bisexual, queer, and/or transgender, they are 8 times more likely to attempt suicide if their family is not supportive.[45] We all want to be loved to our core and when essential parts of our identity, like our sexual orientation and gender identification, are rejected by those we love, that is a deeply painful wound.

So if you see a person belonging to a minority community struggling, reach out. Don't perpetuate the shame that they have likely already endured. Let them know that you care about them and that you want to help them however best you can. And share with them about what you have learned thus far. There are so many resources to support minority populations and this book includes resources for you. Providing these valuable people with the support they need is so necessary. We know that less than 50% of people with a serious mental condition get the help that they need and minority populations are even less likely to receive services. Let's work together to change that statistic.

When it Comes to Acquaintances and Strangers

One of the most awkward situations is when it seems like someone you know clearly has a problem but you're not close enough to talk about it with them. This is a tricky situation. But the reality is, you can't help every person you come in contact with and chances are, the person is much less likely to be open to a conversation about mental health if they're not already close with you.

There are a few questions I ask myself before I reach out to someone regarding their mental health:

1. Do I know their name?
2. Have I talked/texted them in the past week?
3. Do I know something about this person that the rest of the world wouldn't necessarily know?
4. Have I known them longer than a month?
5. Have I seen a change in this person that is concerning to me?

If you answered "no" to most of these questions, chances are, talking to them about their mental health is much too personal. Depression, anxiety, and the other conditions we talked about are very private experiences and expecting someone to disclose to you before you have a solid relationship is asking too much.

So even if you see a classmate, coworker, or stranger on the street showing signs of struggling, be cautious about approaching them. They may be that much more defensive with you because they don't know you very well, and after all, almost all of us feel like we have an image to uphold. What you can do instead, especially if you are really concerned? You can talk to the school counselor or the Human Resources department. You can make a confidential report and then you can know that you have reached out to someone who can appropriately talk with the person.

Of course, you can always get to know that person better. Once you've established a relationship, the person may be more open to hearing your thoughts. However, you don't want to form connections with people solely for the sake of telling them that you are worried about them. If you want to get to know someone, learn about them because you are genuinely interested in spending time with them.

Is there someone that I'm concerned about even though I'm not very close with them? Why am I concerned about that?

_____

_____

What can I do to help that person?

_____

_____

You also should know that as hard as this may sound, you cannot save everyone. It's not humanly possible. We see hurt and suffering on a daily basis. Whether it's the woman without a home asking for money or the man gambling all night at the casino, there are people who face daily challenges. We cannot help every person that we meet or that we see. While we can hope that those people have someone in their lives who cares about them, the best thing we can do is continue to care passionately about the people in our lives that we do know and love. We need to continue leaning into those relationships and hope that our loved ones would be willing to reach out for us as well.

And even though you cannot save everyone that you see hurting, you can still be intentional about helping. You can volunteer with different charities that serve those with mental health disorders, start a kindness campaign at your school (I love Random Acts of Kindness), or be a part of peer counseling club with your classmates. You can participate in walks that fundraise money for those with mental health problems and you can donate money to charities that help those with debilitating setbacks. You can write cards to veterans with PTSD and you can tutor kids who have learning disabilities. You can even become a therapist if you're so inclined! There are countless ways that you can give back to the mental health community and invite you to take part in this.

What are three ways that I can give back to the mental health community?

1. _____

2. _____

3. _____

The Stages of Change

As much as we help (and let's never stop helping), change is a very personal process. Everyone goes at their own pace. I thought it would be helpful to highlight here the Stages of Change so that you can see how change is a gradual process.[46] We often hope that our conversations will provide instantaneous improvements but change usually doesn't happen overnight.

STAGES OF CHANGE

Image credit to The Homeless Hub

A person usually goes through the experiences of pre-contemplation, contemplation, and preparation before they are truly ready to enact change. And much of the time, a person will relapse or slip up, having to repeat the cycle—multiple times. This Stages of Change model does not just apply to substance use, it also applies to medication cooperation with mental disorders like schizophrenia and bipolar disorders as well. This even applies to things like losing weight and exercising more! We learn as we go and each time we get a little bit smarter. No person is perfect nor should they be expected to understand the best response to their problems on the first go-round. This is helpful to remember both for your own struggles and when you see others enduring hardships. Be patient in the process and trust that we are all going at the pace that we can manage for the time being.

Is there anything in your life that you feel like you need to change? Where do you think you fall in the Stages of Change?

_____

_____

What can you do to move to the next phase in the Stages of Change?

_____

_____

Is there anyone in your life that you think needs to make a positive change? What change do they need to make and where do you think they fall in the Stages of Change?

_____

_____

What do you think would help them move to the next phase in the Stages of Change?

_____

_____

Is there a way that you can help them?

_____

_____

Taking Steps Towards Self-Care

While it is important to seek help when you are struggling, one of the best things you can do for yourself is take preventative steps to protect your wellbeing. We call this self-care. While sometimes we feel guilty or shunned for taking time for ourselves, it is critical that you nourish yourself. When we don't prioritize our needs, our wellbeing suffers and as a result, others suffer as well. When we are pushed to our limits, we may have a shorter temper, we are less productive, and it is harder for us to engage with others. Therefore, when we engage in self-care we are ultimately caring for others as well.

Have you noticed that when you're preparing to takeoff in an airplane the flight attendant demonstrates how to use the oxygen mask? They always say to put your own oxygen mask on first before helping someone else. This is exactly how self-care works. We need to invest in our well-being in order to help others.

What exactly is self-care? It's anything that you love to do! What makes you feel recharged, well rested, and happy? I especially love how Dr. Mihaly Csikszentmihalyi conceptualizes self-care with the notion of "flow." Flow is the optimal state when we are so in the moment that we lose track of time.[47] The activity is so emotionally stimulating and engaging that we don't care what other priorities we have on our list. And if you're not sure what you love to do or when you are in "flow?" Follow your natural curiosity and talent and see what you find. Be willing to experiment with your creativity and be open to new experiences.

When do you feel like you are in a state of flow? (Dancing, playing baseball, surfing, etc.)

_____

_____

Let's first see how your current self-care regimen is. This is an awesome assessment from Saakvitne, Pearlman & Staff and I love completing this a few times a year to check in with myself.[48] Why don't you give it a try?

Using the scale below, rate the following areas in terms of frequency within the past six months:

5= Frequently
4=Occasionally
3=Rarely
2=Never
1=It Never Occurred to Me

Physical Self-Care

_____ Eat regularly (breakfast, lunch, dinner)
_____ Eat healthy meals

_____ Exercise

_____ Get regular medical care for prevention

_____ Get medical care when needed

_____ Take time off when needed

_____ Get massages

_____ Dance, swim, walk, run, play sports, sing, or some other physical activity that is fun

_____ Get enough sleep

_____ Wear clothes you like

_____ Take vacations

_____ Take day trips or mini-vacations

_____ Make time away from phone/social media

_____ Other:

Where do you think you excel in this category? Why?

_____

_____

Where do you struggle within this category? What do you think you can do to improve?

_____

_____

Psychological Self-Care

_____ Make time for self-reflection

_____ Have your own personal therapy

_____ Write in a journal

_____ Read literature that is unrelated to school or work

_____ Do something at which you are not expert or in charge

_____ Decrease stress in your life

_____ Let others know different aspects of you

_____ Notice your inner experience—listen to your thoughts, judgments, beliefs, attitudes, and feelings

_____ Engage your intelligence in a new area (art museum, history exhibit, sporting event, theater performance)

_____ Practice receiving from others

_____ Be curious

_____ Say "no" to extra responsibilities sometimes

_____ Other:

Where do you think you excel in this category? Why?

_____

_____

Where do you struggle within this category? What do you think you can do to improve?

_____

_____

Emotional Self-Care

_____ Spend time with others whose company you enjoy

_____ Stay in contact with important people in your life

_____ Give yourself affirmations, praise yourself

_____ Love yourself

_____ Re-read your favorite books, re-watch your favorite movies

_____ Identify comforting activities, objects, people, places, and seek them out

_____ Allow yourself to cry

_____ Find things that make you laugh

_____ Express any frustration in social action, letters and donations, marches, protests

_____ Play with children

_____ Other:

Where do you think you excel in this category? Why?

_____

_____

Where do you struggle within this category? What do you think you can do to improve?

_____

_____

Spiritual Self-Care

_____ Make time for reflection

_____ Spend time with nature

_____ Find a spiritual connection or community

_____ Be open to inspiration

_____ Cherish your optimism and hope

_____ Be aware of nonmaterial aspects of your life

_____ Be open to not knowing

_____ Speak with people who are wise and inspirational

_____ Identify what is meaningful to you and notice its place in your life

_____ Meditate

_____ Pray

_____ Sing

_____ Have experiences of awe

_____ Contribute to causes in which you believe

_____ Read inspirational literature or watch inspirational talks

_____ Other:

Where do you think you excel in this category? Why?

_____

_____

Where do you struggle within this category? What do you think you can do to improve?

_____

_____

Academic, Workplace or Professional Self-Care

_____ Take breaks during the day
_____ Take time to chat with classmates or co-workers
_____ Make quiet time to complete tasks
_____ Identify projects or tasks that are exciting and rewarding
_____ Set limits with the people in your life
_____ Balance your schedule so that no one day or part of the day is "too much"
_____ Arrange your work/study space so it is comfortable and comforting
_____ Talk with a mentor
_____ Ask for what you need in order to perform/feel better
_____ Other:

Where do you think you excel in this category? Why?

_____

_____

Where do you struggle within this category? What do you think you can do to improve?

_____

_____

Balance:

_____ Strive for balance within your school/work life and daily routine

_____ Strive for balance among work, family, relationships, play, and rest

Overall, how do you think you are doing in terms of self-care after doing this test?

_____

_____

What are the biggest roadblocks in your life that prevent you from self-care?

_____

_____

How will you overcome these challenges so that you can make self-care a daily priority?

_____

_____

Once you start getting in the habit of self-care, you'll see how much fun it is. You'll quickly see the benefits and not only will you begin to feel happier, the people around you will feel more positive as well. Our emotions are contagious and that works in either direction. When you are stressed, you're more likely to snap at others, complain, and just be generally unpleasant. This permeates to others and they either will start to avoid you or join in with the whining. But if you are feeling well-rested, you're more likely to meet the day with optimism, kindness, and a can-do mentality. Others will gravitate towards your goodwill and they will feel better just by being around you.

What are some different things that you can do for self-care? I'm listing a plethora of options for you here. *Go ahead and circle all the ideas that sound appealing to you.*

Self-Care Set

Hold, walk, or play with your pet ~ Go for a bike ride ~ Sing in the car ~ Visit the water ~ Let go of something ~ Drink something warm ~ Be alone ~ Watch a funny video ~ Eat dessert ~ Travel to a new country ~ Unplug from your phone ~ Take a walk ~ Plant something ~ Take a bath ~ Cook a delicious meal ~ Take a nap ~ Spend time with loved ones ~ Read a book ~ Lose track of time ~ Forgive yourself ~ Visit a Farmer's Market ~ Learn something new ~ Try a new hobby ~ Create something ~ Watch a movie ~ Meet someone that inspires you ~ Organize your space ~ Watch a sunset ~ Give and get hugs ~ Write in a journal ~ Meet with a therapist ~ Wander around town ~ Meditate ~ Write a sincere note to someone ~ Get a massage ~ Call a friend ~ Speak kindly to others ~ Engage in small acts of kindness ~ Go for a hike ~

Sit outside ~ Light a candle ~ Take a yoga class ~ Dance ~
Drive somewhere unknown ~ Bake a treat you love ~ Visit
a park ~ Paint a picture ~ Go for a run ~ Watch a show
~ Write a poem~ Buy some flowers ~ Practice gratitude
~ Watch the clouds ~ Stretch ~ Watch some Netflix ~
Sit in the sun ~ Wear an outfit that you feel great in ~
Cuddle up in a blanket ~ Decorate your space ~ Watch
sports ~ Breathe fresh air ~ Pray ~ Chat with a friend
~ Drink plenty of water ~ Listen to a podcast ~ Do a
crossword puzzle ~ Work on a puzzle ~ Play Sudoku ~
Spend time with kids ~ Volunteer ~ Go shopping ~
Plan a vacation ~ Go swimming ~ Play an
instrument ~ Sleep in ~ Visit family ~
Celebrate important milestones ~ Laugh ~ Step away
from work ~ Go to a comedy show ~ Use a coloring
book ~ Knit ~ Visit an art museum ~ Go to a concert
~ Play on Pinterest ~ Sleep eight hours ~ Play video
games ~ Plant a garden ~ Clean your space ~
Join an intramural team ~ Visit a spiritual place
~ Clean out your inbox ~ Get a haircut ~
Build something ~ Make your bed ~ Sit by a
fireplace ~ Compliment someone ~
Give someone a gift ~ Do what you loved as a
kid ~ Listen to the sounds of nature ~

What activities stand out for you? Why?

_____

_____

What activities would you like to start implementing in your life?

_____

_____

Self-care is a commitment. It's easy to say that you will start adding these different ideas to your routine but if you don't create a plan, it won't happen. You need to be proactive with your self-care and actually pencil it in your schedule, just as you would with class assignments and work deadlines. My recommendation is that you pick at least one self-care item per day each week. If you're smart with your planning, you can incorporate multiple things that you love into one activity. Therefore, a self-care schedule for the week might look like this:

Monday: Take a yoga class. Drink plenty of water afterward.

Tuesday: Watch a movie with friends after studying together. Eat some popcorn.

Wednesday: Listen to a Ted Talk while getting ready for the day. Cook dinner with mom.

Thursday: Go for a hike after class with sister.

Friday: Watch the football game. Go to the dance afterward and see friends. Wear a favorite outfit that I feel confident in.

Saturday: Sleep in and have an amazing breakfast. Go window-shopping and play video games for an hour after getting some work done.

Sunday: Play a board game with the family. Listen to favorite playlist then read a new book.

Why don't you give it a try?

Monday: _____

Tuesday: _____

Wednesday: _____

Thursday: _____

Friday: _____

Saturday: _____

Sunday: _____

Many people think self-care is simple and some even scoff at why we "waste time" talking about self-care. Well, if everyone were so great at it, then we wouldn't need to take the time to talk about self-care. But clearly, people are not prioritizing their mental and physical health and they develop short and long-term problems as a result. In fact, those who are burdened by anxiety and stress have a decreased capacity to remember information in their long-term memory and thus have a harder time on their exams, even if they earned good grades during the year.[49] If we're not careful, negative experiences like these can build up and it can make it easier for depression to surface. We have to be intentional about our wellbeing. Tough circumstances are bound to be a part of our life so we have to come back with self-care that much harder. For every negative experience we have, we need to have at least three positive experiences to make up for it.[50]

It's clear that self-care is the secret for not only having wellbeing today, but for years to come. It's best to develop the habit of practicing self-care now rather than putting it off for later. But you need to give yourself grace as you learn the art of wellbeing. Many people engage in all or nothing thinking when it comes to daily self-care. They either work tirelessly and never give themselves a break or they veg out all day (or week) and are unable to accomplish anything. The trick is finding that sweet spot where you are still able to complete assignments and finish tasks while still having some fun. Some days it will be easier to find this sense of balance but when you do have an off balance day, remember that you can always have a fresh start tomorrow.

Mindfulness Matters

It's so important to listen to your body. It will give you important clues about how you are feeling. When we ignore the pangs of our body, whether they are signaling hunger, anger, or chaos, our body can ricochet out of control. Especially for children and young adults, the body has a very physical reaction to stress. It is not uncommon that students will say they have headaches, stomachaches, or general pain when they are feeling overwhelmed.[51]

Do you experience any physical symptoms when you're stressed?

_____

_____

A way to center and ground ourselves, especially when our body is feeling out of control, is to practice mindfulness. Mindfulness is the conscious awareness of our current thoughts, feelings, and environment along with an acceptance of this awareness that is open, curious, and nonjudgmental.[52] It can make all the difference. One study, involving two groups of healthy people, taught one group how to practice mindfulness by focusing on the breath. After just three months of implementation, the mindful group showed a 44% decrease in psychological distress, a 46% decrease in illnesses like colds and headaches, and a 24% decrease in the stress response to every day struggles. The other group showed no such changes.[53] And mindfulness is especially great for those feeling depressed. A study of teenagers who had depression were taught how to practice mindfulness three times per day and their anxiety and depression were significantly reduced while their self-esteem and sleep quality improved.[54]

A lot of us feel intimidated by the concept of mindfulness. We think that we have to sit quietly for hours each day or go to India like Elizabeth Gilbert did in *Eat Pray Love*. This doesn't have to be the case, though. I'm a big fan of Goldie Hawn's book because her title suggests all that we need: just *Ten Mindful Minutes* a day. It doesn't need to dominate your life or change your routine. Instead it helps you step away from your stress momentarily, coming back recharged and refocused. You can choose a set time of day that you practice mindfulness or you can intersperse it throughout your week at different times. There are many different things that you can do to be mindful, but the classic activity is finding a quiet place, either closing your eyes or resting them on a set point, and focusing on your breath. That's it. Pay attention to the in and out of your breath. You can rest your hands on your belly and feel your stomach rising and falling with each breath. Your mind will naturally wander but you want to keep pulling your attention back to your breath.

Ten minutes can feel like a long time at first. Even starting with three minutes of stillness can be a great beginning. Research has found that what strengthens the brain and wellbeing is not how long you meditate but how often you practice throughout the day.[55] My motto (not only with mindfulness but with most things): *some is better than none*. Taking just a few minutes to be mindful is better than none at all. And if the silence is too much? You can listen to some peaceful music. My favorite way to practice mindfulness is through a guided meditation app on my phone. I recommend the Calm App. It's a great guide because you can choose the background sound (I love the sound of rain or ocean waves) and you can pick how long you want to meditate and what you'd like the topic to be on. you'd like the topic to be on. Apps like these have a range of choices including a focus on calmness, happiness, managing stress, or gratitude—you name it! Most also track your progress and how many minutes/days that you meditate so it's nice to see how you're doing.

And maybe sitting still is too hard for you—that's alright. Try a yoga, pilates, or tai chi class. Anything that helps you focus on your body, its movement, and the breath are all excellent grounding activities. Going to a class just once a week can help you find your center once more. Of course, you have to find what feels best for you, but any activity that includes mindful movement is undeniably good for your mental health. The most important thing is that you treat yourself kindly as you try a mindful practice. It takes diligence and the more often you give it a try, the easier it will be. Be patient as you learn.

What do you think of mindfulness? Do you think this is something that would help you?

_____

_____

What roadblocks would get in your way of practicing mindfulness?

_____

_____

What goal(s) can you set regarding the implementation of mindfulness in your life?

_____

_____

Sleep Counts

It's also worth noting how integral your sleep is. While there are many things that you can do for self-care, sleeping must come as a staple. Without sleep, it's nearly impossible to accomplish tasks successfully, let alone enjoy life. Snoozing is one of those things that you must be unapologetically prioritize. And while every person is a little different, most young adults need an average of eight to nine hours of sleep each night to function at their best.[56] The statistics say that most teens get about seven hours of sleep so this is something that we can all work on.

When we go without sleep, whether we stay up late watching our favorite show or we pull an all-nighter cramming for an exam, we develop a "sleep debt." This is when our body and brain function insufficiently because we owe it hours of sleep. The only way we can payback this sleep debt is by sleeping back the hours that we missed.[57] As I'm yawning typing this section, I'm realizing that I have my own sleep debt to pay. And while we may brush it off and think it's not a big deal, sleep is not something to underestimate.

In fact, sleep problems may increase the risk for certain mental conditions or they may result from a diagnosis. Sleep problems are especially prevalent with depression, anxiety, bipolar disorder, and ADHD. The good news is that when we prioritize our sleep, many of the symptoms that go along with a disorder may subside.[58] In fact, one study looked at Prisoner of War victims and followed them for 37 years. They found that the soldiers who acquired enough sleep had the greatest amount of mental resilience.[59] This shows how reparative sleep can be. Whether we've had a bad day or endured a traumatic experience, the brain repairs itself during sleep.

If you're struggling with sleep, it's important to develop sleep hygiene. What are some ways that you can settle down to sleep?[60]

Maintain a regular sleep schedule // Exercised on a regular basis // Avoid smoking
Keep the bedroom dark at night // Keep a TV out of the bedroom // Drink tea
Listen to guided meditation // Try deep breathing // Avoid caffeine in the evening
Keep your phone away // Use a sound or white noise machine // Keep the room cool
Use a mattress and pillow you like // Wear an eye mask // Use ear plugs // Read a book
Take a bath // Don't look at the clock // Write in your journal // Wear nice pajamas

Circle any ideas that you think might help you.

How many hours of sleep would you say you get each night on average? _____

How is your sleep? Is this a strength in your life or something that you need to work on?

_____

_____

If you need to improve your sleep habits, what can you do to implement a better sleep routine?

_____

_____

Healthy Eats and Staying Hydrated

Just as important as sleep, it's so necessary that you make an effort to eat a healthy diet. So many of us are so busy all the time that we grab what's convenient—no matter how many calories are in it. Or we're on such a tight budget that we get what's cheapest (like the drive through) rather than spend a little more on organic produce and fresh ingredients. And let's be honest, sometimes junk food can be downright delicious. Who doesn't love a slice(s) of pizza or an ice cream? I have a major sweet tooth and a day without sugar is just a little unimaginable to me. Can you relate to any of this?

This isn't a book solely about nutrition where I'm trying to tell you exactly what to eat. But I am trying to write about mind and body balance. In order to feel our best mentally and physically, we have to give our body the nutrients that it needs. Our brain is working constantly (even while we sleep), and the only way it can run properly is if it has enough nutrients from the foods we eat.

In fact, research has shown that when we ingest a diet high in refined sugars there is impaired brain function and there is also a correlation with depression.

So, while you can still indulge and have that cookie every now and then (because you deserve a treat sometimes!) it's important for us to be mindful about what we are putting into our bodies. You don't have to make seismic shifts in your diet. But maybe you can start adding a salad for lunch or eating some vegetables at dinner. Perhaps you can try taking a vitamin (they even make adult gummies now) or you can eat an orange with your breakfast. You can get creative and try different types of cuisines for different healthy flavors—Thai, Indian, Lebanese—you never know what you might like. In fact, we know that those who eat a "traditional diet" which includes Mediterranean cuisine (think olive oil, fresh fruits/vegetables, nuts, and fish) have a 25% to 35% lower chance of developing depression. We also know that when people take probiotics (think Greek yogurt) their anxiety level, perception of stress, and mental outlook improve compared to people who don't take probiotics.[61]

How would you describe your diet? Would you say you eat healthily or is it something you can improve on?

_____

_____

And let's not forget about water. It seems like such a no-brainer, but without water, we can't function. In fact, did you know that the average human can't live more than three days without water?[62] Even when we are mildly dehydrated, studies show that our mood decreases.[63] On top of this, when we are dehydrated our attention span is impaired along with our memory and motor skills (meaning, how fast we can move our bodies).[64] [65] Water has a profound impact on our lives and it even effects our day-to-day as well. For example, one study found that students who brought water to their exams performed better.[66]

How much water should you be drinking? There are some different opinions, but most researchers recommend the 8 X 8 rule: eight 8-ounce glasses per day.

How many glasses of water do you drink per day on average? _____

One way to help inform a more balanced diet (including how much water we drink) is by coming up with a game plan. When you've set some goals about how you would like to eat and drink, you're more likely to follow along with the schedule. Now you'll notice I'm not setting any weight loss goals and I'm not trying to restrict anything from my diet. When we feel punished (like when we tell ourselves: No more chocolate!) our body usually rebels. We only have self-control for so long before we lose it. But when we approach healthful eating with moderation, our goals are much more attainable. And start with where you're at. I will be honest in saying that nutrition is not one of my strengths. I tend to be on the go and I eat whatever is convenient. Instead of pretending that I'm a guru in this area, I'm being realistic with what is attainable at this time. Here are three of my nutrition goals that I'm working on currently:

1. Eat three forms of fruits or vegetables a day.
2. Take a vitamin each day, including B-12 for energy support.
3. Drink eight glasses of water per day.

What are three nutrition goals that you have?

1. _____

2. _____

3. _____

Something else that I recommend is that you start taking ownership of your food. I'm guessing that as a child, the adults in your life usually prepared food for you or you went out for meals. But as you get older, learning how to cook your own food can be an incredibly fun skill to develop. I wish that I started cooking at a younger age (maybe I would be decent at it by now!) but the challenge of picking out a recipe, getting the ingredients, and putting it all together (especially with someone you enjoy spending time with) can be a great way to wind down from the day. Cooking really is an art form and it's not an ability that you develop overnight. But with dedicated effort, you'll see how rewarding it is when you gradually improve. Have a family member teach you the classic family recipes and watch some cooking shows. Go on Pinterest or go to the bookstore and get a cookbook. You can get creative with this and I think you'll be surprised by how much you might enjoy it.

What recipes do you want to learn how to cook?

_____

_____

Remember to Play

Cooking is a form of playing. When we can get lost in an activity and lose track of time, we are in full play-mode. Remember how much you loved to play when you were a kid? Maybe you loved playing softball or dressing up dolls. Or you would finger paint all day and then meet up with your neighborhood friends for a game of hide-and-seek. Children are in a state of "flow" so much of the time because they are so actively engaged in their play activities.

What did you like to play when you were a kid?

_____

_____

One of my great concerns is that technology is robbing us of our ability to play. While adults seem to grow out of play (unfortunately), even kids nowadays are losing their ability to play. It is much more rare to see a kid riding their bike or shooting hoops than it is to see them absorbed in an iPad or checking their fantasy football league. Blame it on our phones, our laptops, and our TVs, but regardless of the source, we are struggling to engage one another. All these hours that are spent in front of screens (which amounts to nine full years for the average 65-year-old) are kidnapping us from connecting with one another and simply playing.[67]

So what can we do? We have to walk away from the screens sometimes. We have to find our inner child and play once more. We need to be willing to be silly—to look stupid even—and to just let go of any preconceived notions of how we "should" behave. Maybe it's tapping into what you loved as a kid once more. Or maybe it's trying something entirely new that is just now sparking your curiosity. Find some time to carve out to re-enter into this youthful spirit—you'll be able to laugh so much more and just be present in those moments. It's even better if you can spend time with others while playing. Maybe it's a board game, going on a scavenger hunt, or playing laser tag. Be creative!

What can do to add more play into your life?

_____

_____

_____

And of course, I'm not banning all technology. You'll notice in the Self-Care Set that I do include things like Netflix, video games, and going on social media because you may find it really enjoyable at times. Just make sure it's not the *only* thing you do for self-care.

Self-care can be your best defense for protecting your wellbeing. We all will inevitably feel stressed and overworked at times, no matter how hard we try to implement self-care, but we can still seek balance. You deserve to have joy, fun, and laughter in your life. You only get this day, at this age, in this year, and it's right in front of you. You might as well enjoy it! I hope that you'll start treating yourself with kindness and giving yourself the love you deserve. And if you feel guilty about investing in yourself? Remember that when you take care of yourself, you are ultimately taking care of others as well. When you nurture your best self, you have your best self to give.

Wellbeing Within

Everything that we've discussed so far is irrelevant unless you value one thing: yourself. If you don't foster a love for yourself and what you stand for, all of the knowledge, self-care, and resources are meaningless. I cannot make you care about yourself: only you can do that. Of course I can tell you that you are valuable, worthwhile, and loved but only you can believe that.

Can I ask something of you? I know you might have doubts about yourself; perhaps you think you aren't "enough," but will you do something for me? Will you read the following sentence and truly believe it?

I am enough.

Write it down: _____

You are enough. I am enough. Just as we are. Do you believe this? Life is going to be a long journey if you cannot start accepting yourself for the imperfectly perfect person that you are. We all have made mistakes and we will continue to do so. That is the essence of being human. But it is also the essence of humanness that includes goodness, compassion, and kindness. I believe that you already possess all that inherit goodness within you. You just have to own that and know that you are entirely wonderful.

Write down five qualities that you have that are AMAZING.

1. _____
2. _____
3. _____

4. _____

5. _____

Many of my clients speak words of shame to themselves. I often hear the following come out of their mouth on a weekly basis:

- I'm not smart enough.
- I'm not talkative enough.
- I'm not pretty/handsome enough.
- I'm not funny enough.
- I'm not cool enough.
- I'm not thin/strong enough.

The list could go on and on. But let's stop this list. Rather than compare ourselves to others, let's remember that we are enough as we are. It's not about comparison. There can be room for everyone to succeed. I know that I have days when I definitely feel insufficient, and days when I have doubts, but I have to remind myself: I am enough. And if someone thinks that I am not enough? Then that is their loss and someone else's gain. I trust that even when someone says "no" to me or denies me an opportunity, something better is meant to come along. I believe this for your life as well.

Engage Your Optimism

While I don't believe that we should ever fake happiness, I do believe that we can choose optimism. Happiness is a feeling, but optimism is a perspective. Even if you are having a bad day, bad week, bad month, or a bad year, you can still choose to see the light in even the darkest situation.

I was reminded of this just the other day in my own life. I had a brand new (used) car that I was so excited about—I'd had it for just a week. Within that week, the car had a window smashed in and my testing kit for school (which was worth over $500) was stolen from the car. I was shocked and disappointed. I felt betrayed that someone out there could do such a thing and I felt dismayed. Not only would it be $800 to have the window replaced, I also had to pay for the $500 testing kit. But somehow, my classmates found out about my situation and completely unknowingly, they surprised me later that week with the nicest note and over $300 to help me pay back the testing kit. *Wow.* What an incredible act of human kindness. They had tuition bills, rent, and all kinds of other payments just like me and yet, they humbly offered me this incredible help to make up for my loss.

It would be so easy to be brought down by the break-in and wallow in my disappointment. But instead, my feelings of gratitude and love surmount any sadness I could have had. My classmates showed me that goodness does trump evil and while bad things do happen, there is always something more positive to pay attention to.

Is there a situation in your life where you could have been brought down but you choose instead to see the positive?

_____

_____

_____

_____

Choosing optimism is a decision that provides lifelong benefits. In fact, optimists tend to live 19% longer than pessimists.[68] And during that lifetime, optimistic people tend to have longer and more satisfying relationships, a larger number of friends, more energy, the ability to make more money, a more successful career, more fruitful social interactions, and better physical health.[69]

That's nothing to scoff at. In effect, maintaining a positive attitude supports the "broaden-and-build" theory, where a sense of optimism broadens our perspective and thus helps us build a better life.[70]

We need to be intentional about our optimism. It is not something to be taken lightly (no pun intended). Those who are pessimists are eight times more likely to become depressed.[71] Many think this negativity is inborn: they believe they were born negative, sarcastic, or cynical. Pessimistic teens are more likely to believe that negative comments made about them are a sign that they are truly worthless, rather than just serving as someone's opinion.[72]

This pessimistic attitude is not cemented in our personalities, though. We know that the human brain is very malleable and our neurons are constantly re-wiring depending on the activities that we engage in. This concept of neuroplasticity has a tremendous effect and has found support in just one of many studies. Dr. Martin Seligman from the University of Pennsylvania conducted a 30-year study where he showed that 10-year-old children can be taught how to practice optimism, and as a result, their chances of developing depression during adolescence were greatly reduced.[73]

I especially love how Dr. Seligman points out these essential differences between optimists and pessimists:[74]

- A *pessimist* makes it **personal** by saying: "It's all my fault," while an *optimist* makes it **impersonal** by saying, "I didn't have control over this so I am not to blame."
- A *pessimist* thinks **permanently** by saying: "It's always like this," while an *optimist* thinks about the **impermanent** by saying, "I'm going through a tough time, I know it will get better."
- A *pessimist* believes it is **pervasive** by saying: "Everything is terrible," while an *optimist* sees the **specifics** by saying, "This certain thing is hard for me, but the rest of my life is still good."

Based on these examples, do you think you have the mentality of a pessimist or an optimist?

_____

_____

How can you think more positively?

_____

_____

_____

Practice Gratitude

If you're having a hard time implementing this idea of optimism, I always think the best place to start is with gratitude. When I am working with my clients who are severely depressed and/or anxious, we always camp out at gratitude. Researchers have found that 90% of people are happier, 84% have less stress and depression, and 78% have more energy when they practice gratitude.[75] In fact, being thankful adds an average of seven years to our lives![76] Practicing thankfulness is a reminder that no matter how dark your life may seem, there is still a glimmer of goodness somewhere. I love this chart from Happier Human—I think it perfectly demonstrates just how vast and expansive gratitude is when it comes to impacting our happiness.

Image credit to Amit Armin, HappierHuman.com

Gratitude takes a deliberate, conscious effort, though. For so many of us, gratitude comes up about once a year when the turkey is going around the table. I call this the Thanksgiving talk of gratitude. We say what we're thankful for once, almost as an obligatory measure, and then let's add some stuffing and mashed potatoes to our plates. If we want to see our optimism and joy in life truly spike up, we need to make gratitude more of a daily experience. This takes effort and if you're not already practicing this, it will take some time before it feels habitual. Again, this is where neuroplasticity comes in so handy. When you take 21 days to practice something, your neurons (brain cells) will start to synch into the routine. Thus, practicing gratitude over time will start to feel more organic and natural to you. So, how do we do this?

It's what I like to call the Five Daily Gratitudes. Every day, either before you go to bed or when you wake up in the morning, write down five things that you're thankful for within the 24-hour period. I recommend getting a journal to keep all your notes in the same place. These Gratitudes don't have to be major, life changing things. They can be simple. The goal is that you start looking around your world to see the goodness that still exists. You may have to search for it, but you'll see how much more rewarding your life will feel when you take time to do this.

I notice that my clients who implement this see some major changes. First, they say that their perspective feels different. Rather than focusing on the negatives in their lives (and let's be real, the negative will always be there), they choose instead to search for the positive factors in their life. One of my favorite authors, Shawn Achor, talks about this idea and shared a study that followed participants who wrote down good things each day for a week. The study found that these participants were happier and less depressed not only at the one-month, three-month, and six month follow-ups; they were also more optimistic after they stopped the exercise entirely.[77] Therefore, the benefits of daily gratitude are long lasting and far-reaching.

Another change that my clients experience after practicing the Five Daily Gratitudes is that they feel more resilient. They see how strong they are and they begin to recognize how they have overcome challenges. As time goes on, you will see that things can improve and that bad situations don't have to last forever. It will get better. As you start to see your list of gratitude get longer and longer, you'll begin to see that your life is even more fulfilling and rewarding than you probably realized. So no matter how bad it might seem for a little while, the Five Daily Gratitudes give you an opportunity to notice how many amazing people and experiences you have in your life.

Another awesome thing about trying this out? Your life will feel so much more complex and defined. So many of us just get through our days and the memories fly out the window. I mean seriously, do you remember what you did last Tuesday? How was last February for you? Don't feel alone if nothing comes to mind. Unless you have a life-changing event (good or bad), your life can start to feel pretty monotonous. The Five Daily Gratitudes is a great way to buffer your memory. The brain is triggered by written memories so this is essentially a journal that documents the blissful bites of your life. It's a gift to give to yourself someday. You can look back and see that the Tuesdays, Thursdays, and other weekdays of your life weren't so boring after all. They were actually quite complex with inside jokes, meaningful relationships, and unexpected occurrences. Take the time to jot it down—it takes just about five minutes.

I'll give you an example by writing out my Five Daily Gratitudes right now. As I'm writing this chapter, it's Wednesday, December 28, 2016. What I am thankful for today?

1. My Siamese kitten sleeping beside me: One of the greatest joys in my life has been getting a kitten. I've wanted one forever and seeing him right next to me is the happiest feeling in the world.
2. A day at home in pajamas: Let's be real—I'm a homebody. Whenever I get to be home in my pajamas, it's a special treat. I guess that's an introvert for you.
3. A new planner: I love getting to decorate my planner before the start of a new year.
4. Trying a new restaurant: One of my favorite things about things about living in LA is that there are so many amazing places to eat. Last night we tried an Italian restaurant and it was just incredible. Spaghetti and meatballs for life.
5. Taking a bath: My cousin gave me the best Lush bath bombs for Christmas and treating myself to a bath is a nice way to unwind during the holidays.

It's just five things—nothing major. The five things that I listed were simple little moments in my life that were happy nonetheless. Why don't you give it a try?

What are your Five Daily Gratitudes?

1. _____

2. _____

3. _____

4. _____

5. _____

It's so important to be mindful about our gratitude. We have to try that much harder to be positive because the human brain caters to negativity. Think about it; you've had an incredible day—everything has gone right. You feel confident, your teacher or boss commends you on your work, and you even get asked out on a date. And then you find out that someone didn't like your idea for the group project. Or you gained a few pounds. Or a friend didn't laugh at your joke. Suddenly, the day feels shot. Have you had this experience before? Somehow, we can have ten great things happen in a day and just one bad thing sets the scale completely off. How does that happen?

One way to combat this is by focusing on the Five Daily Gratitudes. That doesn't mean that you ignore your problems, but you don't have to focus on those problems for an unnecessary amount of time. We can be mindful about balancing our brain's internal scale by magnifying the good in our lives and minimizing the negative.

Own Who You Are

For some of us, it's easier to feel off-kilter when it comes to this mental scale. It can take just one bad experience or hurtful person to make us feel utterly shattered. And while you need to process the pain that comes from that, you also have to realize that no one should be able to rob you of your inner essence. You have incredible gifts, talents, and intricacies that make you the person that you are.

As much as people may try to hurt you, you have to choose whether or not you are going to let them win. Are you going to let people take away your confidence, your character, and your contributions? People can always intimidate you if you let them.

Take this very moment to realize that you don't have to do that. You don't have to let people silence your ideas. You don't have to let fear cripple you from taking action or from speaking up. It's time to own who you are. Remember how I told you that you are enough? You truly are. You are skilled enough, you are smart enough, you are dedicated enough to accomplish what you are seeking to do. If you compare yourself to others, we all will fall short in one way or another. So instead, hold yourself to your own highest standard and seek to meet that potential. That's all that you owe to yourself.

One way I like to get myself pumped up, especially when I'm feeling inferior, is to give myself some positive affirmations. The words that we read are words that we receive. Be mindful of what you are choosing to take in. I used to love how my best friend Abbie would put all kinds of positive affirmation posters around her apartment to lift her spirits. She was applying to dozens of medical schools and she was so afraid that it wouldn't work out. But all the time, she would read these positive words— brushing her teeth, making her dinner, getting ready for her interviews. Those positive words made her believe in herself. You bet that was evident when she went in for her interview at UCLA medical school. They could sense her poise, her dedication, and her intentionality. They offered her a spot and she's now in her second year of medical school there.

Don't underestimate the impact that these words can have on your life. Some people roll their eyes when it comes to affirmations— they don't think it has any real effect. It doesn't if you don't believe it. And sure, it's not a magical cure-all that solves every problem that we have. But it can change our attitude and our motivation. If you start to believe the affirmations that you are reading and saying— they can have a life changing impact. People will sense your new-found energy and motivation and that has a magnetic effect. And more than anything, you will likely feel capable of setting out for what you want to achieve, despite the fear. As Buddha says: "What we think, we become."

That is not to say that you won't feel afraid. Some of the greatest goals that are worth accomplishing have a tremendous amount of trepidation attached. Just take writing this book—I certainly feel fear as I'm typing out the chapters. I could stop myself every day if I started wondering what people will think and who will criticize it. I could fill in all the usual comparisons—I'm not smart enough, not a good enough writer, not knowledgeable enough to have anything to contribute. But I am leaning into this challenge regardless of my fear, because I believe that I do have something valuable to offer and hopefully someone out there will benefit by reading it. That is enough for me.

What are some affirmations that you can tell yourself? I'll share some of the greats with you and then I'll write down some of my own affirmations. I love all work by Louise Hay.[78] Here are some of my favorites by her:

1. I am willing to see my magnificence.
2. I no longer judge or criticize myself. I am free to love who I am.
3. Healing means to make whole and to accept all parts of myself—not just the parts I like, but all of me.
4. I am an open channel for creative ideas.
5. I feel safe in the rhythm and flow of my ever-changing life.

Some of my affirmations that I wrote include:

1. I deserve to feel joy, gratitude, and wonder in my life.
2. I can help someone today. I have something valuable to contribute.
3. I am filled with loving kindness towards others and myself.
4. My life is filled with beautiful blessings that I can enjoy every day.
5. Everything will turn out as it meant to be. I am right where I belong.

As you can see, affirmations are incredibly personal. They evolve over time depending on the stage of your life. All that matters are that these words uplift you. Take some time to find five affirmations that you gravitate towards. Pinterest has wonderful life quotes and again, Louise Hay's website (http://www.louisehay.com/affirmations/) is filled with gems of inspiration.

What are five affirmations that you connect with?

1. _____
2. _____
3. _____
4. _____
5. _____

And sometimes, the most powerful words are the ones that are written by you.

Write down five of your own personal affirmations.

1. _____
2. _____
3. _____
4. _____
5. _____

You can make beautiful posters of these words or you can look for images online that inspire you. You can make a journal, hang up the quotes around your room, and text these positive messages to friends. Get creative with this! *Take the space below to create an artistic design of one your affirmations:*

My Hope for You

I can't believe that we are already coming to the end of our time together! I hope that as you read this page you are walking away with a greater understanding about mental health, both for your own life and to help others as well. My sincere wish for you is that you learned how to ask for help if you need it and that you learned how to have conversations with others that you care about. Mental health is both a personal experience and a shared one—we greatly impact others and they have a tremendous effect on us as well. The best way we can love one another and ourselves is to be intentional about looking out for each other. It's naming it when we see or feel a concern. It's facing it when we or someone we know needs help. It's embracing it when we finally learn that we are enough as we are—when we finally know that we are worthy and deserving of love—just as others are as well.

I know this book can take you on an emotional roller coaster. Whether you knew it or not, your life has probably been touched by mental health in some way long before you knew the definitions, symptoms, or warning signs of any mental health condition. I hope this book is providing you with a sense of empowerment and ownership now that you have learned more. The best thing you can do is equip yourself with knowledge. Even if you are tempted to look the other way or avoid the problems of your life or someone else's, lean into it instead. Find your inner Harry Potter and fight the Voldemorts in your life. Don't let mental health scare you. You can win the battle and you can help others win theirs as well.

Be an advocate for mental health. Take the pledge to stand up against the stigma. There is no shame in seeking resources or talking about mental health. In fact, it is the brave and strong person who can do so.

I thank you for sharing this journey with me. It has been such a privilege writing this book. I am so passionate about mental health—especially for young adults—because I believe that we can be the ones to turn the tide. All the whispers, all the gossip, all the secrets about mental health (and especially mental illness)—I believe that we can be the ones to finally bring a positive voice to it. We are not afraid; we stand together in this fight. We can and will overcome. I am standing alongside you.

Let this book serve as a launching point for you as you begin to learn more. Take these words and let them guide you to other resources. Wherever your curiosity has been sparked—follow that. Spend time volunteering and getting to know the people who live with these experiences. Hear their stories, straight from them. They are people just like you and me and they are just as deserving of an incredible life. They, we, you, me—we are all enough.

I'm sending all my best to you and I wish you wellness always.

With love,

Lauren

Resources that You Can Rely On

It can feel so overwhelming when you're learning about mental health and different disorders for the first time. You may not always know who to turn to for help. Here are some resources to help you take the next steps—either towards getting help for yourself or someone you love.

Emergency Situations

If you are in an emergency and need immediate help, always **call 911**.

National Suicide Prevention Hotline
1-800-273-8255

I'm Alive
Website to immediately chat: https://hopeline.com/
1-800-784-2433

The Jedd Foundation
Text "Start" to 741-741
Call: 1-800-273-8255
https://www.jedfoundation.org/mental-health-resource-center/

American Foundation for Suicide Prevention
https://afsp.org/

Adolescent Suicide Hotline
800-621-4000

National Organization for People of Color Against Suicide
http://nopcas.org/
973-204-8233

Gay & Lesbian Trevor Help Line Suicide Prevention
http://www.thetrevorproject.org/
1-800-850-8078

Therapy Resources

GoodTherapy.org: Find the Right Therapist
http://www.goodtherapy.org/

National Alliance on Mental Illness (NAMI)
HelpLine: 800-950-6264
Email: info@nami.org
Website: http://www.nami.org/

Psych Central: Find a Therapist
http://psychcentral.com/find-help/
1-800-843-7274

Mental Health America
http://www.mentalhealthamerica.net/

Text, Talk, Act
http://www.creatingcommunitysolutions.org/texttalkact
Text FAMILY to 89800 and then receive a series of text messages that guides your family through a conversation about how they can support each other

Treatment Advocacy Center
http://www.treatmentadvocacycenter.org/
703-294-6001

If You're in Middle School or High School

Minding Your Mind
http://mindingyourmind.org/

Bring Change 2 Mind
http://bringchange2mind.org/
415-814-8846

Society for Adolescent Health and Medicine
http://www.adolescenthealth.org/Home.aspx
847-686-2246

Teen Mental Health.org
http://teenmentalhealth.org/

If You're in College

Active Minds
202-332-9595
http://activeminds.org/

American College Counseling Center
http://www.collegecounseling.org/

American College Health Association
https://www.acha.org/

ULifeline
http://www.ulifeline.org/

Anxiety and Obsessive Compulsive Disorders

Anxiety Resource Center
http://anxietyresourcecenter.org/
616.356.1614

Panic Disorder Information Hotline
800- 64-PANIC

The TLC Foundation for Body-Focused Repetitive Behaviors
https://www.bfrb.org/
831-457-1004

Depressive Disorders

Anxiety and Depression Association of America
https://www.adaa.org/
240-485-1001

Depression and Bipolar Support Alliance
http://www.dbsalliance.org/
(800) 826-3632

International Bipolar Foundation
http://ibpf.org/
(858) 598-5967

Psychotic Disorders

Schizophrenia and Related Disorders Alliance of America
http://www.sardaa.org/
Call-in information: (855) 640-8271
Entry code: 88286491#

Feeding and Eating Disorders

National Association of Anorexia Nervosa and Associated Disorders
http://www.anad.org/
Helpline: 630-577-1330

National Eating Disorders Association
http://www.nationaleatingdisorders.org/
800-931-2237

Eating Disorders Center Hotline
1-888-236-1188

Overeaters Anonymous
https://oa.org/
505-891-2664

Substance Use Disorders

Alcoholics Anonymous
http://www.aa.org/

Narcotics Anonymous
https://www.na.org/

Drug & Alcohol Treatment Hotline
800-662-HELP

Addiction Center: Guiding You From Rehab to Recovery
24/7 Treatment Help: 877-830-2915
https://www.addictioncenter.com/teenage-drug-abuse/

The National Center on Addiction and Substance Abuse
http://www.centeronaddiction.org/
212-841-5200

National Institute on Alcohol Abuse and Alcoholism
https://www.niaaa.nih.gov/

National Institute on Drug Abuse
https://www.drugabuse.gov/

Substance Abuse and Mental Health Services Administration
https://www.samhsa.gov/
1-877-726-4727

Al-Anon Family Groups

http://al-anon.alateen.org/

757-563-1600

Developmental Disorders

Children & Adults with Attention Deficit/Hyperactivity DisorderHotline

1-800-233-4050

National Center for Learning Disabilities

http://www.ncld.org/

1-888-575-7373

Child Mind Institute

http://childmind.org/

212-308-3118

Understood: for Learning and Attention Issues

https://www.understood.org/en

Other Helpful Numbers

Child Abuse Hotline

800-4-A-CHILD

Gay & Lesbian National Hotline

1-888-THE-GLNH (1-888-843-4564)

Rape (People Against Rape)

1-800-877-7252

Rape, Abuse, Incest, National Network (RAINN)

1-800-656-HOPE (1-800-656-4673)

National Institute of Mental Health
https://www.nimh.nih.gov/index.shtml

Brain and Behavior Research Foundation
https://bbrfoundation.org/
800-829-8289

Suggested Readings

Behind Happy Faces: Taking Charge of Your Mental Health
Ross Szabo and Melanie Hall

Better than Before: Mastering the Habits of Our Everyday Lives
Gretchen Rubin

College of the Overwhelmed: The Campus Mental Health Crisis and What to Do About It
Richard Kadison and Theresa Foy Digeronimo

Coping with Moods: Young Adult's Guide to the Science of Health
Jean Ford

Daring Greatly: How the Courage to be Vulnerable Changes the Way We Live, Love, Parent, and Lead
Brene Brown

Happy at Last: The Thinking Person's Guide to Finding Joy
Richard O'Connor

Loving Someone with Anxiety: Understanding and Helping Your Partner
Kate N. Thieda

Ten Mindful Minutes: Giving Our Children—and Ourselves the Social and Emotional Skills to Reduce Stress and Anxiety for Healthier, Happier Lives
Goldie Hawn with Wendy Holden

The Anxiety Survival Guide for Teens: CBT Skills to Overcome Fear, Worry, and Panic
Jennifer Shannon

The Beauty Myth: How Images of Beauty are Used Against Women
Naomi Wolf

The Center Cannot Hold: My Journey through Madness
Elyn R. Saks

The Happiness Advantage: The Seven Principles that Fuel Success and Performance at Work
Shawn Achor

Welcome to the Jungle: Everything You Wanted to Know about Bipolar Disorder but Were Too Afraid to Ask
Hilary T. Smith

When Nothing Matters Anymore: A Survival Guide for Depressed Teens
Bev Cobain

Acknowledgements

There have been significant people in my life who have always encouraged me and supported me no matter what. Writing a book takes a lot of gumption and on the days when I feel doubtful, there are certain people who are always in my corner. I know authors usually wait until the end of their acknowledgements to thank the most integral people in their lives but I want to start off my thanks by recognizing them first.

To my mom and dad, thank you for always looking out for me. You've fostered a fearlessness in me—to always reach higher and dream bigger. I can't thank you enough for always having faith in me. All of the prayers and support has made all the difference in my life and I am who I am today because of you. I love you both so much.

I also want to thank my partner, Greg. We're coming up on seven years together and we have grown up side by side. You have shown me what hard work and humility looks like and I admire you so much. You are the kindest person I know and getting to share my life with you is the ultimate gift (apart from the incredible gift of our Siamese kitten).

I also want to thank my Auntie Nette who is my mentor and guardian angel (from Santa Rosa!) Thank you for always caring about the happenings in my life—you make me feel so loved. Your Godliness and grace is exemplary and you are such a role model of compassion to me. I cherish the time we have together always.

I also want to thank the friends in my life who have given me such tremendous joy over the years. Lauren, you are my dearest friend and being your Maid of Honor was one of the greatest gifts of my life thus far. And many thanks to your husband (still exciting to say that!), Travis, for his endless help with headshots, book designs, and all kinds of creative projects over the years. You two are a perfect couple.

Many thanks as well to my dear friends Abbie and Kelly, my two beloved Chi Omega sisters. We are always laughing and I treasure our time—especially when it's at Cheesecake Factory. Much love as well to Hannah and Alexis. You two are some of the smartest and loveliest gals that I know and being in your company is to know wisdom.

I also have so many thanks towards National Charity League. I would not have the opportunity to write this book and travel the country had it not been for NCL. I loved my time as Ticktocker and getting to speak about happiness and now mental health is a dream come true. I am honored to be surrounded by such incredible women.

Thanks as well to the Chi Omega community. Because I said yes to Chi Omega my freshmen year at UCLA, amazing adventures have ensued. I met my best friends, I met Greg, and I got to travel as a National Consultant all because of that Bid Day. I look forward to a lifelong experience continuing to support Chi Omega. Owl I'll always be loyally yours.

And to all the educators along the way who have made all the difference. From high school to UCLA, from USC to Pepperdine, there have been fantastic educators who have shown me what passionate academia looks like. You have spent countless hours teaching me and my classmates how we can be most effective in the field of psychology and for this I am truly grateful. I also want to extend a sincere thanks to La Vie Counseling Center, my first training site for offering therapy to clients. It was during this year that I fell in love with the art of therapy and while I have so much to learn, you will always have been the first to show me the way.

It's not just today as I'm writing this section that I'm aware of the many blessings in my life. It's every day that I want to be mindful of this gratitude. Life would be meaningless without the people who matter in my life and I am forever thankful for you all.

Endnotes

1   Major depression among adolescents. *National Institute of Mental Health*. Retrieved from https://www.nimh.nih.gov/health/statistics/ prevalence/major-depression-among-adolescents.shtml

2   Live and thrive: Children and teens. *Anxiety and Depression Association of America*. Retrieved from https://www.adaa.org/living-with-anxiety/ children

3   The top mental health challenges facing students. *Best colleges. com*. Retrieved from http://www.bestcolleges.com/resources/top-5- mental-health-problems-facing-college-students/

4   What is mental health? *Mentalhealth.gov*. Retrieved from https://www. mentalhealth.gov/basics/what-is-mental-health/

5   Saks, E. (2008, August 12). *The center cannot hold: My journey through madness*. New York: Hyperion.

6   Hawn, G., & Holden, W. (2011). *10 Mindful Minutes: Giving Our Children-- and Ourselves--the Social and Emotional Skills to Reduce St ress and Anxiety for Healthier, Happy Lives*. Penguin.

7   How emotionally intelligent are you? Mind Tools. Retrieved from https://www.mindtools.com/pages/article/ei-quiz.htm

8   American Psychiatric Association. (2013). *DSM 5*. American Psychiatric Association.

9   Gmelch, W. H. (1983). Stress for success: How to optimize your performance. *Theory into practice, 22*(1), 7-14.

10 Major depression among adolescents. *National Institute of Mental Health*. Retrieved from https://www.nimh.nih.gov/health/statistics/ prevalence/major-depression-among-adolescents.shtml

11 The top mental health challenges facing students. *Best colleges. com*. Retrieved from http://www.bestcolleges.com/resources/top-5- mental-health-problems-facing-college-students/

12 Neumark Sztainer, D. (2005). I'm, Like, SO Fat! New York: The Guilford Press. pp. 5.

13 Eating Disorders Coalition. (2016). Facts About Eating Disorders: What The Research Shows.http://eatingdisorderscoalition.org.s208556. gridserver.com/couch/uploads/file/fact-sheet_2016.pdf

14 Ulfvebrand, S., Birgegard, A., Norring, C., Hogdahl, L., & von Hausswolff-Juhlin, Y. (2015). Psychiatric comorbidity in women and men with eating disorders results from a large clinical database. *Psychiatry Research*, 230(2), 294-299.

15 The Renfrew Center Foundation for Eating Disorders, Eating Disorders 101 Guide: A Summary of Issues, Statistics and Resources, 2003.

16 Arcelus, J., Mitchell, A. J., Wales, J., & Nielsen, S. (2011). Mortality rates in patients with anorexia nervosa and other eating disorders: a meta-analysis of 36 studies. Archives of General Psychiatry, 68(7), 724-731.

17 Sullivan, P. (1995). American Journal of Psychiatry, 152 (7), 10731074.

18 Eating disorder statistics & research. *Eating Disorder Hope*. Retrieved from https://www.eatingdisorderhope.com/information/statistics-studies

19 The National Institute of Mental Health: Eating Disorders: Facts About Eating Disorders and the Search for Solutions. Pub No. 01-4901. Accessed Feb. 2002. www.nimh.nih.gov/health/publications/eating-disorders-new-trifold/index.shtml

20 National Eating Disorders Association website. Statistics: Eating Disorders and Their Precursors. Accessed feb.2012 http://www.nationaleatingdisorders.org/uploads/statistics_tmp.pdf

21 DeWit, D. J., Adlaf, E. M., Offord, D. R., & Ogborne, A. C. (2000). Age at first alcohol use: a risk factor for the development of alcohol disorders. *American Journal of Psychiatry*, 157(5), 745-750.

22 Drug addiction risk factors. Mayo Clinic. Retrieved from http://www.mayoclinic.org/diseases-conditions/drug-addiction/basics/risk-factors/con-20020970

23 LGBTQ. National Alliance on Mental Illness. Retrieved from https://www.nami.org/Find-Support/LGBTQ

24 Teen drug abuse. Addiction Center. Retrieve from https://www.addictioncenter.com/teenage-drug-abuse/

25 Binge drinking. Addiction Center. Retrieve from https://www.addictioncenter.com/college/binge-drinking/

26 Yanes, A. (2014, April 18). Just say yes? The rise of 'study drugs' in college. CNN. Retrieved from http://www.cnn.com/2014/04/17/health/adderall-college-students/

27 The effects of Adderall use. Drugabuse.com. Retrieved from http:// drugabuse.com/library/the-effects-of-adderall-use/

28 How common is autism? Autism Science Foundation. Retrieved from http://autismsciencefoundation.org/what-is-autism/how-common-is-autism/

29 How common is ADHD? WebMD. Retrieved from http://www.webmd. com/add-adhd/guide/adhd-how-common#1

30 Just how common is ADHD? ADDitude. Retrieved from http://www. additudemag.com/adhd/article/688.html

31 The link between teen drug use and suicide. Teen Rehab Center. Retrieved from https://www.teenrehabcenter.org/resources/drugs-and-suicide/

32 Lambert, Michael J., and Dean E. Barley. "Research summary on the therapeutic relationship and psychotherapy outcome." *Psychotherapy: Theory, research, practice, training* 38, no. 4 (2001): 357.

33 Babyak, M., Blumenthal, J. A., Herman, S., Khatri, P., Doraiswamy, M., Moore, K., ... & Krishnan, K. R. (2000). Exercise treatment for major depression: maintenance of therapeutic benefit at 10 months. *Psychosomatic medicine, 62*(5), 633-638.

34 Depression and anxiety: Exercise eases symptoms. Mayo Clinic. Retrieved from http://www.mayoclinic.org/diseases-conditions/ depression/in-depth/depression-and-exercise/art-20046495

35 Hillman, C. H., Erickson, K. I., & Kramer, A. F. (2008). Be smart, exercise your heart: exercise effects on brain and cognition. *Nature reviews neuroscience, 9*(1), 58-65.

36 Antidepressant medications for children and adolescents: Information for parents and caregivers. National Institute of Mental Health. Retrieved from https://www.nimh.nih.gov/health/topics/child-and-adolescent-mental-health/antidepressant-medications-for-children-and-adolescents-information-for-parents-and-caregivers.shtml

37 Pargament K. The psychology of religion and coping: theory, research, practice. New York: Guilford, 1997.

38 Tepper L, Rogers SA, Coleman EM et al. The prevalence of religious coping among patients with persistent mental illness. PsychiatrServ 2001;52:660-5.

39 Smith TB, McCullough ME, Poll J. Religiousness and depression: evidence for a main effect and the moderating influenceof stressful life events. Psychol Bull 2003;129:614-36.

40 What does "suicide contagion" mean, and what can be done to prevent it? U.S. Department of Health & Human Services. Retrieved from https://www.hhs.gov/answers/mental-health-and-substance-abuse/what-does-suicide-contagion-mean/index.html

41 Crisis on campus: The untold story of student suicides. CDS College Degree Search. Retrieved from http://www.collegedegreesearch.net/student-suicides/

42 Suicide prevention: How to help someone who is suicidal and save a life. HelpGuide.org. Retrieved from http://www.helpguide.org/articles/suicide-prevention/suicide-prevention-helping-someone-who-is-suicidal.htm

43 The teen brain: Still under construction. National Institute of Mental Health. Retrieved from https://www.nimh.nih.gov/health/publications/the-teen-brain-still-under-construction/index.shtml

44 Mental health and minorities: The numbers don't lie. Birmingham Maple Clinic. Retrieved from http://www.birminghammaple.com/11590/bmc-blog/mental-health-and-minorities-the-numbers-dont-lie/

45 LGBTQ. National Alliance on Mental Illness. Retrieved from https://www.nami.org/Find-Support/LGBTQ

46 Stages of Change. The Homeless Hub. Retrieved from http://homelesshub.ca/toolkit/subchapter/stages-change

47 Csikszentmihalyi, M. (1996). Flow and the psychology of discovery and invention. *New Yprk: Harper Collins.*

48 Saakvitne, K. W., Pearlman, L. A., & Abrahamson, D. J. (1996). *Transforming the pain: A workbook on vicarious traumatization.* New York: WW Norton.

49 Hawn, G., & Holden, W. (2011). *10 Mindful Minutes: Giving Our Children--and Ourselves--the Social and Emotional Skills to Reduce St ress and Anxiety for Healthier, Happy Lives.* Penguin.

50 Fredrickson, B. L., & Kurtz, L. E. (2011). Cultivating positive emotions to enhance human flourishing. *Applied positive psychology: Improving everyday life, health, schools, work, and society, 35-47.*

51 Wolfenden, E. (2011, May 4). Physical symptoms of stress in college students. Livestrong.com. Retrieved from http://www.livestrong.com/article/77136-physical-symptoms-stress-college-students/

52 Hawn, G., & Holden, W. (2011). *10 Mindful Minutes: Giving Our Children--and Ourselves--the Social and Emotional Skills to Reduce St ress and Anxiety for Healthier, Happy Lives.* Penguin.

53 Kabat-Zinn, J. (2003). Mindfulness-based interventions in context: past, present, and future. *Clinical psychology: Science and practice, 10*(2), 144-156.

54 Biegel, G. M., Brown, K. W., Shapiro, S. L., & Schubert, C. M. (2009). Mindfulness-based stress reduction for the treatment of adolescent psychiatric outpatients: A randomized clinical trial. *Journal of consulting and clinical psychology, 77*(5), 855.

55 Tang, Y. Y., Ma, Y., Wang, J., Fan, Y., Feng, S., Lu, Q., ... & Posner, M. I. (2007). Short-term meditation training improves attention and self-regulation. *Proceedings of the National Academy of Sciences, 104*(43), 17152-17156.

56 Sleep in adolescents (13 to 18 years). *Nationwide Children's*. Retrieved from http://www.nationwidechildrens.org/sleep-in-adolescents

57 Dement, W. Sleepless at Stanford: What all undergraduates should know about how their sleeping lives affect their waking lives. (1997, September). Retrieved from https://web.stanford.edu/~dement/sleepless.html

58 Sleep and mental health. Harvard Health Publications. Retrieved from http://www.health.harvard.edu/newsletter_article/Sleep-and-mental-health

59 Sleep and mental health. *Sleep Health Foundation*. Retrieved from http://www.sleephealthfoundation.org.au/more/sleep-blog/402-sleep-and-mental-health.html

60 Twelve simple tips to improve your sleep. *Healthy Sleep*. Retrieved from http://healthysleep.med.harvard.edu/healthy/getting/overcoming/tips

61 Selhub, E. (2015, November 16). Nutritional psychiatry: Your brain on food. *Harvard Health Publications*. Retrieved from http://www.health.harvard.edu/blog/nutritional-psychiatry-your-brain-on-food-201511168626

62 Binns, C. (2012, November 30). How long can a person survive without water? Live Science. Retrieved from http://www.livescience.com/32320-how-long-can-a-person-survive-without-water.html

63 Armstrong, L. E., Ganio, M. S., Casa, D. J., Lee, E. C., McDermott, B. P., Klau, J. F., ... & Lieberman, H. R. (2012). Mild dehydration affects mood in healthy young women. *The Journal of nutrition, 142*(2), 382-388.

64 Kempton, M. J., Ettinger, U., Foster, R., Williams, S. C., Calvert, G. A., Hampshire, A., ... & Smith, M. S. (2011). Dehydration affects brain structure and function in healthy adolescents. *Human brain mapping, 32*(1), 71-79.

65 Adan, A. (2012). Cognitive performance and dehydration. *Journal of the American College of Nutrition, 31*(2), 71-78.

66 Tamarkin, S. (2015, January 6). 34 proven ways water makes you awesome. *Greatist.* Retrieved from http://greatist.com/health/health-benefits-water

67 Television watching statistics. Statistic brain. Retrieved from http://www.statisticbrain.com/television-watching-statistics/

68 Seligman, M. E. (2011). *Learned optimism: How to change your mind and your life.* Vintage.

69 Lyubomirsky, S., King, L., & Diener, E. (2005). The benefits of frequent positive affect: does happiness lead to success?. *Psychological bulletin, 131*(6), 803.

70 Fredrickson, B. L. (2001). The role of positive emotions in positive psychology: The broaden-and-build theory of positive emotions. *American psychologist, 56*(3), 218.

71 Scheier, M. F., & Carver, C. S. (1993). On the power of positive thinking: The benefits of being optimistic. *Current Directions in Psychological Science, 2*(1), 26-30.

72 Hawn, G., & Holden, W. (2011). *10 Mindful Minutes: Giving Our Children--and Ourselves--the Social and Emotional Skills to Reduce Stress and Anxiety for Healthier, Happy Lives.* Penguin.

73 Park, N., Peterson, C., & Seligman, M. E. (2004). Strengths of character and well-being. *Journal of social and Clinical Psychology, 23*(5), 603-619.

74 Seligman, M. E. (2011). *Learned optimism: How to change your mind and your life.* Vintage.

75 Hawn, G., & Holden, W. (2011). *10 Mindful Minutes: Giving Our Children--and Ourselves--the Social and Emotional Skills to Reduce Stress and Anxiety for Healthier, Happy Lives.* Penguin.

76 The 31 benefits of gratitude you didn't know about: How gratitude can change your life. Happier Human. Retrieved from http://happierhuman.com/benefits-of-gratitude/

77 Achor, S. (2011). *The happiness advantage: The seven principles of positive psychology that fuel success and performance at work.* Random House.

78 Hay, L. Affirmations. Retrieved from http://www.louisehay.com/affirmations/

About the Author

Photo Credit: Travis Christian

Lauren Cook speaks nationally about mental health and wellness around the country, especially for young adults and their families. She is also the author of *The Sunny Side Up: Celebrating Happiness*. Lauren completed her undergraduate education at UCLA and continued onto USC for her Master's in Marriage and Family Therapy. She is currently at Pepperdine University for her Doctorate in Clinical Psychology. She enjoys working as a Life Coach in her free time. Lauren has interned at NBC Network News, E! News, and Disney ABC Television Group during her time in college. She is a former Miss Teen California and is a passionate advocate for the American Cancer Society. As a sorority alumna of Chi Omega, she enjoys volunteering on the National Recruitment Team and serves as a Recruitment Advisor for the UCLA chapter. She currently lives in Los Angeles with her Siamese cat, Mochi.

For inquiries or to book Lauren for a speaking event, please contact **CAMPUSPEAK** at http://www.campuspeak.com/ or 844-745-8570.

To learn more, please visit:

Lauren's Website:
www.thesunnygirl.com

Lauren's Facebook:
https://www.facebook.com/TheSunnyGirlLaurenCook/

Lauren's Twitter:
https://twitter.com/TheSunnyGirl5

Lauren's Instagram:
https://www.instagram.com/thesunnygirl5/

CPSIA information can be obtained
at www.ICGtesting.com
Printed in the USA
FSOW04n1334030417
32660FS